R Web Scraping Quick Start Guide

Techniques and tools to crawl and scrape data from websites

Olgun Aydin

BIRMINGHAM - MUMBAI

R Web Scraping Quick Start Guide

Commissioning Editor: Amey Varangaonkar
Acquisition Editor: Noyonika Das
Content Development Editor: Kirk Dsouza
Technical Editor: Shweta Jadhav
Copy Editor: Safis Editing
Project Coordinator: Hardik Bhinde
Proofreader: Safis Editing
Indexer: Priyanka Dhadke
Graphics: Alishon Mendonsa
Production Coordinator: Arvindkumar Gupta

First published: October 2018

Production reference: 1301018

Published by Packt Publishing Ltd.
Livery Place
35 Livery Street
Birmingham
B3 2PB, UK.

ISBN 978-1-78913-873-3

www.packtpub.com

To my partner, Joanna Wrobel; my mother, Nejla Aydin; and my father, Fuat Aydin.

– Olgun Aydin

`mapt.io`

Mapt is an online digital library that gives you full access to over 5,000 books and videos, as well as industry leading tools to help you plan your personal development and advance your career. For more information, please visit our website.

Why subscribe?

- Spend less time learning and more time coding with practical eBooks and Videos from over 4,000 industry professionals

- Improve your learning with Skill Plans built especially for you

- Get a free eBook or video every month

- Mapt is fully searchable

- Copy and paste, print, and bookmark content

Packt.com

Did you know that Packt offers eBook versions of every book published, with PDF and ePub files available? You can upgrade to the eBook version at `www.packt.com` and as a print book customer, you are entitled to a discount on the eBook copy. Get in touch with us at `customercare@packtpub.com` for more details.

At `www.packt.com`, you can also read a collection of free technical articles, sign up for a range of free newsletters, and receive exclusive discounts and offers on Packt books and eBooks.

Contributors

About the author

Olgun Aydin is a PhD candidate at the Department of Statistics at Mimar Sinan University, and is studying deep learning for his thesis. He also works as a data scientist.

Olgun is familiar with big data technologies, such as Hadoop and Spark, and is a very big fan of R. He has already published academic papers about the application of statistics, machine learning, and deep learning.

He loves statistics, and loves to investigate new methods and share his experience with other people.

I would like to thank my partner, Joanna Wrobel, for her unlimited support and patience in the process of writing this book.

About the reviewer

Ezgi Nazman is a Research Assistant in Gazi University, Statistics where she has been studying for a PhD since 2015. She did her bachelor's degree at Ege University, Statistics in 2012. She was Erasmus student in University of Hradec Kralove, Informatics and Management between September 2011 - June 2012. From 2013-2015, she studied Master of Science in Statistics, Gazi University.

Her research interests lie in the area of statistics, data mining, and machine learning, ranging from theory to implementation. She has had five articles published on SCI and other international indexes, and eight presented papers in international conferences. She is one of the authors of a book titled *Arastirmacilar icin SPSS Uygulamali Deney Tasarimi*.

I would like to thank the project coordinator, Hardik Bhinde, for his kind and helpful instructions during this book's review process.

Packt is searching for authors like you

If you're interested in becoming an author for Packt, please visit `authors.packtpub.com` and apply today. We have worked with thousands of developers and tech professionals, just like you, to help them share their insight with the global tech community. You can make a general application, apply for a specific hot topic that we are recruiting an author for, or submit your own idea.

Table of Contents

Preface

This book is for R programmers looking to quickly get started with web scraping. Some fundamental knowledge of R is required. This book will give you a quick, hands-on introduction to web scraping and how to use popular R libraries, such as `rvest` and RSelenium. Right from the initial environment setup to quickly scraping HTML web pages for useful information, this book will cover only the absolute fundamentals of web scraping without going into too much depth. By the end of the book, you will have the understanding that's necessary for scraping any web page using R programming.

Who this book is for

This book is for R programmers looking to quickly get started with web scraping, as well as data analysts who want to learn about scraping using R. Some fundamental knowledge of R is all that is required to get started with this book.

What this book covers

Chapter 1, *Introduction to Web Scraping*, introduces web scraping techniques, which are getting more and more popular, since data is as valuable as oil in the 21st century. In this chapter, you can find detailed information about web scraping technologies. We also take an overview of some of the key languages for web scraping, such as XPath and regEX. We'll also look into some web scraping libraries for R, such as `rvest` and RSelenium technologies.

Chapter 2, *Working with the XML Path Language and the Regular Expression Language*, looks at XPath and regEX rules, which are quite important to know when scraping a web page. In this chapter, you can find useful information about these languages and also have a chance to write XPath and regEX rules from scratch.

Chapter 3, *Web Scraping with rvest*, covers the rvest library. Scraping a web page with R is straightforward thanks to the rvest library, which was developed by Hadley Wickham. In this chapter, you can find tips and tricks about the library and learn how to write an R script by using the rvest library to scrape a web page from scratch.

Chapter 4, *Web Scraping with RSelenium*, explores RSelenium. RSelenium is a technology for testing, but it's also useful for scraping web pages. In this chapter, you can find an overview of Selenium and learn how to scrape a web page using RSelenium library.

Chapter 5, *Storing Data and Creating Cronjobs*, deals with the matter of storage. After collecting data, you should store the dataset somewhere; it would be good if you could use a cloud-based solution, such as AWS RDS, EC2, Google Cloud Platform, or Microsoft Azure. Also, if you would like to schedule the collection of data, it's possible to create cronjob that will help you do so. In this chapter, you can find an overview of databases and cloud platforms, and you'll also learn how to connect databases and schedule cronjobs using R.

To get the most out of this book

- To get the most out of this book, its important that you have an idea of what web scraping is. Also, it is advised that you have good hands-on experience with R programming.
- If you have R and RStudio ready on your PC to get started, you will find the information of all packages that are required for scraping data within the chapters.

Download the example code files

You can download the example code files for this book from your account at www.packt.com. If you purchased this book elsewhere, you can visit www.packt.com/support and register to have the files emailed directly to you.

You can download the code files by following these steps:

1. Log in or register at www.packt.com.
2. Select the **SUPPORT** tab.
3. Click on **Code Downloads & Errata**.
4. Enter the name of the book in the **Search** box and follow the onscreen instructions.

Once the file is downloaded, please make sure that you unzip or extract the folder using the latest version of:

- WinRAR/7-Zip for Windows
- Zipeg/iZip/UnRarX for Mac
- 7-Zip/PeaZip for Linux

The code bundle for the book is also hosted on GitHub at https://github.com/PacktPublishing/R-Web-Scraping-Quick-Start-Guide. In case there's an update to the code, it will be updated on the existing GitHub repository.

We also have other code bundles from our rich catalog of books and videos available at https://github.com/PacktPublishing/. Check them out!

Download the color images

We also provide a PDF file that has color images of the screenshots/diagrams used in this book. You can download it here: http://www.packtpub.com/sites/default/files/downloads/9781789138733_ColorImages.pdf.

Conventions used

There are a number of text conventions used throughout this book.

CodeInText: Indicates code words in text, database table names, folder names, filenames, file extensions, pathnames, dummy URLs, user input, and Twitter handles. Here is an example: "Mount the downloaded WebStorm-10*.dmg disk image file as another disk in your system."

A block of code is set as follows:

```
<publisher> (root element node)
<author>J Olgun Aydin</author> (element node)
lang="en" (attribute node)
```

Any command-line input or output is written as follows:

```
install.packages("RPostgreSQL")
```

Bold: Indicates a new term, an important word, or words that you see onscreen. For example, words in menus or dialog boxes appear in the text like this. Here is an example: "Select **System info** from the **Administration** panel."

Warnings or important notes appear like this.

Tips and tricks appear like this.

Get in touch

Feedback from our readers is always welcome.

General feedback: If you have questions about any aspect of this book, mention the book title in the subject of your message and email us at customercare@packtpub.com.

Errata: Although we have taken every care to ensure the accuracy of our content, mistakes do happen. If you have found a mistake in this book, we would be grateful if you would report this to us. Please visit www.packt.com/submit-errata, selecting your book, clicking on the Errata Submission Form link, and entering the details.

Piracy: If you come across any illegal copies of our works in any form on the Internet, we would be grateful if you would provide us with the location address or website name. Please contact us at copyright@packt.com with a link to the material.

If you are interested in becoming an author: If there is a topic that you have expertise in and you are interested in either writing or contributing to a book, please visit authors.packtpub.com.

Reviews

Please leave a review. Once you have read and used this book, why not leave a review on the site that you purchased it from? Potential readers can then see and use your unbiased opinion to make purchase decisions, we at Packt can understand what you think about our products, and our authors can see your feedback on their book. Thank you!

For more information about Packt, please visit `packt.com`.

Introduction to Web Scraping 1

Web scraping is the process of extracting a structural representation of data from a website. The formatting language used to configure data on web pages may display HTML variability, because existing techniques for web scraping are based on markup. A change in HTML can lead to the removal of incorrect data.

Throughout this book, we will be using R to help us scrape data from web pages. R is an open source programming language and it's one of the most preferred programming languages among data scientists and researchers. R not only provides algorithms for statistical models and machine learning methods, but also provides a web scraping environment for researchers. The data collected from websites should also be stored somewhere. For this, we will learn to store the data in PostgreSQL databases, which we will do by using R.

As an example, a company may want to autonomously track product prices for its competitors. If the information does not provide a proprietary API, the solution is to write a program that targets the marking of the web page. A common approach is to parse the web page into a tree representation and resolve it with XPath expressions. If you have any questions like, *Okay how can we make scripts run automatically?* You will find the answer in this book.

The aim of this book is to offer a quick guide on web Scraping techniques and software that can be used to extract data from websites.

In this chapter, we will learn about the following topics:

- Data on the internet
- Introduction to **XPath (XML Path)**
- Data extraction systems
- Web scraping techniques

Learning about data on the internet

Data is an essential part of any research, whether it be academic, marketing, or scientific . The **World Wide Web (WWW)** contains all kinds of information from different sources. Some of these are social, financial, security, and academic resources and are accessible via the internet.

People may want to collect and analyse data from multiple websites. These different websites that belong to specific categories display information in different formats. Even with a single website, you may not be able to see all the data at once. The data may be spanned across multiple pages under various sections.

Most websites do not allow you to save a copy of the data to your local storage. The only option is to manually copy and paste the data shown by the website to a local file in your computer. This is a very tedious process that can take lot of time.

Web scraping is a technique by which people can extract data from multiple websites to a single spreadsheet or database so that it becomes easier to analyse or even visualize the data. Web scraping is used to transform unstructured data from the network into a centralized local database.

Well-known companies, including Google, Amazon, Wikipedia, Facebook, and many more, provide **APIs (Application Programming Interfaces)** that contain object classes that facilitate interaction with variables, data structures, and other software components. In this way, data collection from those websites is fast and can be performed without any web scraping software.

One of the most used features when performing web scraping of the semi-structured of web pages are naturally rooted trees that are labeled. On this trees, the tags represent the appropriate labels for the HTML markup language syntax, and the tree hierarchy represents the different nesting levels of the elements that make up the web page. The display of a web page using an ordered rooted tree labeled with a label is referred to as the **DOM (Document Object Model)**, which is largely edited by the WWW Consortium.

The general idea behind the DOM is to represent HTML web pages via plain text with HTML tags, with custom key words defined in the sign language. This can be interpreted by the browser to represent web-specific items. HTML tags can be placed in a hierarchical structure. In this hierarchy, nodes in the DOM are captured by the document tree that represents the HTML tags. We will take a look at DOM structures while we focus on XPath rules.

Introduction to XPath (XML Path)

An XPath represents a path, and when evaluated on a tree, the result is the node set at the end of any path in the tree. HTML, the formatting language used to configure the data in web pages, aims to create a visually appealing interface.

In particular, **XML Path Language** (**XPath**) provides powerful syntax for handling specific elements of an XML document and, to the same extent, HTML web pages, in a simple way. XPath is defined as a DOM by the World Wide Web Consortium.

There are two ways to use XPath:

- To identify a single item in the document tree
- To address multiple instances of the same item

The main weakness of XPath is its lack of flexibility. Each XPath expression is strictly related to the structure of the web page you are defining.

However, this limitation has been partially reduced since relative road expressions have been added in recent releases. In general, even small changes to the structure of a web page can cause an XPath expression that was defined in an earlier version of the page to not work correctly. In the following screenshot, you can see one XPath rule and its response:

```
> $x('//*[@id="menu-packt"]/span')
< ▼ [span.menu-text] 🔘
    ▼ 0: span.menu-text
        accessKey: ""
        assignedSlot: null
      ▶ attributeStyleMap: StylePropertyMap {size: 0}
      ▶ attributes: NamedNodeMap {0: class, class: class, length: 1}
        autocapitalize: ""
        baseURI: "https://www.packtpub.com/"
        childElementCount: 0
      ▶ childNodes: NodeList [text]
      ▶ children: HTMLCollection []
      ▶ classList: DOMTokenList ["menu-text", value: "menu-text"]
        className: "menu-text"
        clientHeight: 0
```

Data extraction systems

A web data extraction system can be defined as a platform that implements a set of procedures that take information from web sources. In most cases, the average end users of Web Data Extraction systems are companies or data analysts looking for web-related information.

An intermediate user category often consists of non-specialized individuals who need to collect some web content, often non-regularly. This user category is often inexperienced and is looking for simple yet powerful Web Data Extraction software packages. DEiXTo is one of them. DEiXTo is based on the W3C Document Object Model and allows users to easily create inference rules that point to a portion of the data for digging from a website.

In practice, it covers a wide range of programming techniques and technologies such as web scraping, data analysis, natural language parsing, and information security. Web browsers are useful for executing JavaScript, viewing images, and organizing objects in a more human-readable format, but web scrapers are great for quickly collecting and processing large amounts of data. They can display a database of thousands, or even millions, of pages at a time (Mitchell 2015).

In addition, web scrapers can go places that traditional search engines cannot reach. By searching Google for *cheap flights to Turkey*, a large number of flights pop up, including advertising and other popular search sites. Google simply does not know what these websites actually say on their content pages; this is the exact consequence of having various queries entered into a flight search application. However, a well-developed web scraper will know the prices that vary over time of a flight to Turkey on various websites and can tell you the best time to purchase your ticket.

Web scraping techniques

Web scraping techniques automatically open a new world for researchers by automatically extracting structured datasets from readable web content. A web scraper accesses web pages, finds the data items specified on the page, extracts them, transforms them into different formats if necessary, and finally saves this data as a structured dataset.

This can be described as pretending to know how a web browser works by accessing web pages and saving them to a computer's hard disk cache. Researchers use this content for analysis after cleaning and organizing data.

A web scraper reverses the process of manually gathering data from many web pages and putting together structured datasets from complex, unstructured text that spans thousands—even millions—of individual pages. Web scraping discussions often bring with them questions about legality and fair use.

In theory, web scraping is the practice of collecting data in any way other than a program interacting with an API. This is usually accomplished by writing an automated program that queries a web server, which usually requests data and then parses that data to extract the necessary information.

There are a lot of different types of web scraping techniques. In this section, the most popularly used web scraping techniques will be described and discussed.

Traditional copy and paste

Occasionally, due to our process of manual examination, the copy and paste method is one of the best and workable web scraping technologies. However, this is an error-prone, boring, and tiresome technique when people need to scrap lots of datasets (Web scraping, 2015).

Text grabbing and regular expression

This is a simple and powerful approach that's used to obtain information from web pages. This technique is based on UNIX commands or regular expression mapping features of the programming language.

Document Object Model (DOM)

By parsing a web browser such as Internet Explorer or Mozilla browser control, programs can import dynamic content that's been generated by client-side scripting. These browser controls break web pages into a DOM tree based on which programs can take sections of pages.

Semantic annotation recognition

Pages that need to be scraped may contain metadata, semantic marks, or additional explanations that can be used to find specific data snippets. If the annotations are embedded in pages, such as Microformat, this technique is stored as a special case of DOM parsing, and additional annotations that are organized into a semantic layer are stored and managed separately from web pages. Thus, the scraper can get the data schema and instructions of this layer before scraping the pages.

Web scraping tools

It is possible to customize web scraping solutions. There are many software tools that can be used for this. These software tools provide a record interface that automatically recognizes the data structure of a page and removes the need to manually write web scraping code, or provides some script functions and database interfaces that can be used to extract and convert the content. Some of those tools are listed below;

- **Diffbot**: This is a tool that uses computational vision and machine learning algorithms that have been developed for collecting data from web pages automatically, in a behavior like a human being would perform.
- **Heritrix**: This is a web crawler that was designed for web archiving.
- **HTTrack**: This is a web browser that is free and open source, and was initially designed to scrape websites. It can also work offline.
- **Selenium (software)**: This is used for testing the frameworks of web applications.
- **OutWit Hub**: This special scraper is a web scraping application that has built-in data, image, document extractors, and editors that are used for automatic search and extraction.
- **Wget**: This is a computer program that receives content from websites that supports access to websites through HTTP, HTTPS, and FTP protocols.
- **WSO2 Mashup Server**: This tool lets you to gain information based on the web from different sources like web services.
- **Yahoo! Query Language (YQL)**: This is a query-like language similar to that of SQL that lets you query, filter, and join data across web services.

JavaScript tools

It is also possible to use JavaScript for web scraping tasks, mostly used JavaScript frameworks are listed as follows:

- **Node.js**: Node.js is an open source, cross-platform JavaScript environment that allows JavaScript code to run without the need for a web browser.

- **PhantomJS**: PhantomJS is a script-free and headless browser that's used to automate web pages with the JavaScript API that's provided.

- **jQuery**: jQuery is a rich, cross-platform JavaScript library. With jQuery, which is easy to use and learn, it is possible to develop Ajax applications and mark objects in the DOM tree.

Web crawling frameworks

The following can be utilized to build web scrapers:

- **Scrapy**: Scrapy is a free and open source web crawling platform written in Python that was originally designed for scraping the web. It is also possible to use Scrapy as a general purpose web scraping tool if you use its new version and APIs.

- **rvest**: rvest is an R package that was written by Hadley Wickham that allows simple data collection from HTML web pages.

- **RSelenium**: RSelenium is designed to make it easy to connect to a Selenium Server/Remote Selenium Server. RSelenium allows connections from the R environment to the Selenium Webdriver API.

Web crawling environment in R

R provides various packages to assist in web search operations. These include XML, RCurl, and RJSON/RJSONIO/JASONLite. The XML package helps to parse XML and HTML, and provides XPath support for searching XML.

The RCurl package uses various protocols to transfer data, generate general HTTP requests, retrieve URLs, send forms, and so on. All of this information is used for transactions. These processes use the `libcurl` library. JSON is an abbreviation of JavaScript Object Notation and is the most common data format used on the web. Rjson, RJSONIO, and JsonLite packages convert data in R into JSON format.

Web scraping is based on the sum of unstructured data, mostly text, from the web. Resources such as the internet, blogs, online newspapers, and social networking platforms provide a large amount of text data. This is especially important for researchers who conduct research in areas such as Social Sciences and Linguistics. Companies like Google, Facebook, Twitter, and Amazon provide APIs that allow analysts to retrieve data.

You can access these APIs with the R tool and collect data. For Google services, the RGoogleStorage and RogleMap packages are available. The TwitteR and streamR packages are used to retrieve data from Twitter.

For Amazon services, there is the AWS tools package, which provides access to Amazon Web Services (EC2/S3) and MTurkR packages that provide access to the Amazon Mechanical Turk Requester API. To access news bulletins, the GuardianR package can be used. This package provides an interface to the Content API of the Guardian Media Group's Open Platform.

The RNYTimes package on the same shelf also provides broad access to New York Times web services, including researchers' articles, metadata, user-generated content, and offers access to content.

There are also some R packages that provide a web scraping environment in R. In this book, we will also look at two packages that are well-known and used the most: `rvest` and RSelenium.

The `rvest` is inspired by the beautiful soup library, while HTML is a package that simplifies data scraping from web pages. It is designed to work with the `magrittr` package. Thus, it is easy and practical to create web-based search scripts consisting of simple, easy-to-understand parts.

Selenium web is a web automation tool that was originally developed specifically for scraping. However, with Selenium, you can develop web-scavenging scripts. Selenium can also run web browsers. Since Selenium can run web browsers, all content must be created in the browser, which can slow down the data collection process.

There are browsers like `phantomjs` that speed up this process. The RSelenium package allows you to connect to a Selenium Server. RSelenium allows for unit testing and regression testing on a variety of browsers, operating systems, web apps, and web pages.

Summary

In this chapter, we talked about the important rules of RegEx and Xpath. We talked about the general idea of web scraping and web crawling. We then described web scraping techniques, methodologies, and frameworks, before finally introducing the various web scraping environments that are available in R.

In the next chapter, we will learn about XPath rules. We will focus on XPath methodology and how to write XPath rules. We will then learn about the main idea behind these rules and put them into practice. After writing our first RegEx and Xpath rules, we will jump into writing our first web scraper by using R. The RSelenium and rvest libraries are going to be used throughout this book.

2
XML Path Language and Regular Expression Language

XPath primarily handles the nodes of XML 1.0 or XML 1.1 trees. It is used to represent the hierarchical structure of an XML document. XPath uses non-XML syntax and works on the logical structure of XML documents. This structure is also known as the **data model**. XPath is designed to be used embedded into a programming language. It has a natural subset that can be used for mapping.

A regular expression, regex or regexp, represents a search model used in computer science. Regex emerged as a result of the work of the American mathematician Stephen Cole Kleene in the 1950s. It is also being used with Unix text-processing programs. There are different forms of syntax for writing regular expressions: the POSIX standard and Perl syntax. A regular expression in search engines is used in search and replace operations and lexical analysis in text editors. It is possible to use regex in many programming languages, either built-in or through libraries.

In this chapter, we will cover the following topics:

- XML Path (XPath)
- Regular expression language (Regex)
- Exercises on RegEx and XPath

XML Path (XPath)

XPath is a syntax that provides functionality between XSL transformations and XPointer. It deals with parts of an XML document. It is used to manipulate strings, numbers, and Boolean expressions to handle the relevant parts of the XML document. XPath defines the path to a listener for each node type in an XML document. The primary syntactical structure in XPath is the expression. An expression is used to obtain an object that has one of the following four basic types:

- Node-set
- Boolean
- Number
- String

Key words in XPath are not written separately and they are written using lowercase characters. Each node in XML has a unique ID, a typed value, and a string value. Also, some nodes can even have a name. The value written to a node can be zero or atomic value strings. A sequence containing exactly one element is called a **singleton**. An item is identical to a singular sequence containing this item. Names in XPath are called **QNames** and they consist of a namespace, a prefix, and a local name. A QName might be the case of converting a namespace prefix into an expanded QName by resolving it using namespaces statically known to a namespace URI. It contains an expanded name, a custom namespace URI, and a local name. An extended surname also preserves the original namespace prefix as if it were, to make it easier to convert the expanded QName into a string.

In the following part, we will focus on these topics:

- Nodes
- Relationship between nodes

Nodes

XPath has seven different types of nodes: element, attribute, text, namespace, processing-instruction, comment, and document nodes.

Let's talk about the following example of an XML document. This document shows us the XML structure about a product of a publisher; the title of this product is *Quick Start Guide:R*, the author of this product is Olgun Aydin, and the publication date of it is 2018:

```
<?xml version="1.0" encoding="UTF-8"?>
<publisher>
<product>
<title lang="en">Quick Start Guide: R</title>
<author>Olgun Aydin</author>
<year>2018</year>
</product>
</publisher>
```

On following the XML structure, we can see the following types of XML nodes:

```
<publisher> (root element node)
<author>J Olgun Aydin</author> (element node)
lang="en" (attribute node)
```

Relationships between nodes

In XPath, there is a hierarchy between nodes, which helps us to understand the flow in any XML documents. Also, sometimes, we need to be more specific, for example, "Get the attribute class of the div node that is the parent node of span with the items class".

In this part, we will discover the relationship of the nodes: parent, child, sibling, ancestor, and descendant. Also, we will investigate how they look using sample XML documents.

Parent

Each element and attribute should have a parent node.

The following example shows that the product element is the parent of the title, author, and year elements:

```
<product>
  <title>Quick Start Guide: R</title>
  <author>Olgun Aydin</author>
  <year>2018</year>
</product>
```

Child

Parent nodes can have more than one child node. If we would like to call all of the child nodes of the `product` node, there will be `title`, `author`, and `year`, because the these elements are child nodes of the `product` element:

```
<product>
  <title>Quick Start Guide: R</title>
  <author>Olgun Aydin</author>
  <year>2018</year>
</product>
```

Sibling

Nodes that have the same parent node are called `siblings`. The following example code shows that the `title`, `author`, and `year` elements are siblings:

```
<product>
  <title>Quick Start Guide: R</title>
  <author>Olgun Aydin</author>
  <year>2018</year>
</product>
```

Ancestor

The following example code the ancestors of the `title` element are the book element and the `publisher` element.

The structure of the ancestor flows from top to bottom:

```
<publisher>
 <product>
 <title>Quick Start Guide: R</title>
 <author>Olgun Aydin</author>
 <year>2018</year>
 </product>
</publisher>
```

Descendant

The following example code shows that the descendants of the `publisher` element are the `product`, `title`, `author`, and `year` elements.

The structure of the descendant flows the opposite way, that is, from bottom to top:

```
<publisher>
 <product>
 <title>Quick Start Guide: R</title>
 <author>Olgun Aydin</author>
 <year>2018</year>
 </product>
</publisher>
```

XPath is used to select nodes in the XML document to indicate the path expressions of these expressions. The node is selected by following a path or steps. The most useful ways and explanations are given in this table:

Expression	Description
node1	This expression is used for selecting all of the nodes that have the name node1.
/	This expression is used for selecting nodes from the root node.
//	This expression is used to select the nodes in the document from the current node that matches the selection, regardless of where they are.
.	This expression is used for selecting the current node.
. .	This expression is used for selecting the parent node of the current node.
@	This expression is used for selecting attributes.

The following table shows some sample Xpath expressions and the results related to those expressions:

Path Expression	Result
publisher	This expression is used for selecting all nodes that have the name publisher.

/publisher	This expression is used for selecting nodes from the publisher root node.
publisher/product	This expression is used for selecting all of the product elements that are children nodes of the publisher node.
//product	This expression is used to select product nodes in the XML document from the current node that matches the selection, regardless of where they are.
publisher//product	This expression is used for selecting all of the product elements that are descendants of the publisher element.
//@lang	This expression is used for selecting all of the attributes that have namelang.

Predicates

Predicates are for the purpose of finding some specific nodes or any node that contains some specific value. Predicates should be used in square brackets.

The following table shows some sample Xpath expressions and the results related with those expressions:

Path Expression	Result
/publisher/product[1]	This expression is used for selecting first element of product.
/publisher/product[last()]	This expression is used for selecting the last product element.
/publisher/product[last()-1]	This expression is used for selecting the latest product element.
/publisher/product[position()<3]	This expression is used for selecting the first two product elements.

`//title[@lang]`	This expression is used for selecting all of the `title` elements that are with an attribute called `lang`.
`//title[@lang='en']`	This expression is used for selecting all of the title elements that are with an attribute called `lang`, which has the en value.

Selecting unknown nodes

To select `unknown/undefined` nodes, it's good to use wildcards.

The following table shows some sample `Xpath` expressions and the results related to those expressions:

Path Expression	Result
`/publisher/*`	This expression is used for selecting all of the child element nodes of `publisher`.
`//*`	This expression is used for selecting all of the elements.
`//title[@*]`	This expression is used for selecting all of the `title` elements that have at least one kind of attribute.

Selecting several paths

The following table shows some sample `Xpath` expressions and the results related to those expressions:

Path Expression	Result
`//product/title | //product/author`	This expression is used for selecting all of the `title` and price elements

`//title	//author`	This expression is used for selecting all of the `title` and `author` elements
`/publisher/product/title	//author`	This expression is used for selecting all of the `title` elements and all of the `author` elements

Regular expression language (Regex)

Regular expressions are extremely useful when they are used to extract information from any text by searching for a specific sequence of ASCII or Unicode characters. The web is frequently used in search operations. One of the most impressive features of Regex is that it can be used in almost all programming languages. Basically, a regular expression is a formula that helps explain a text. RegEx's name comes from the mathematical theory underlying the idea. It is usually shortened to *regex* or *regexp*.

You can use regular expressions with a text bean that you can usually access using your programming language. If it is known how a Regex engine works, it will be easier to generate regexes. It will be easy to understand why you cannot do what you expect with a regular expression and write more complex expressions.

There are basically only two types of regular expression engines. These are text-oriented and normal-oriented engines. Normal-oriented engines use the regular expression to match the next character in the normal expression. If a match is found, the motor travels normally along the string. If there is no matching, the engine returns to the previous position in the normal expression and to the matrix where it can try a different path.

A text-oriented engine searches the string to try all combinations of the normal expression before proceeding to the next character in the word. Text-oriented engines do not return to the start when searching the symbol. Often, a text-oriented engine finds the same matches as a regular expression engine.

Regex always returns the leftmost match, even if the engine finds a better match later in the search. When a string is applied to a regex, the engine starts with the first character in the string. In the first expression, it refers to all possible permutations of the normal expression.

If all probabilities have been tried and found unsuccessful, the engine continues with the second character in the text. Again, it regularly tests all possible permutations of the normal expression in the same order. The result is that the regex engine returns the left-most match. The regular expression engine works like a normal text search. However, it is important to know which steps the engine follows.

How to match a single character

It is possible to define and use regular expressions with every programming language. Although the use of regular expressions between programming languages is somewhat different, it is often the same.

The dot (.) is used for matching any of characters. When dot is used as a character, the escape character should be used: \. A question mark (?) is used for defining that the preceding character is optional. When it needs to be used as a question mark, an escape character should be used: \?.

How to match the characters of a set

When a set of character wants to be used, they should be used in brackets: [abc]. This regex matches only one of this set of characters. ^. could be used not to match any of the set of characters. [^abc]. matches any of the characters that are not a, b, or c. It is also possible to specify a range [0-9], [a-z] .This regex matches everything in the range. Instead of using [0-9], use the \d and, for [^0-9], this express, \D, can be used.

How to match words

When there is a need to match entire words, single characters and modifiers can be used to repeat a character or a set of character:

- + repeats the preceding character or set of character
- * repeats the preceding character
- {x} is used for defining the exact number of repetitions.

Exercises on RegEx and XPath

In this part, we are going to do some exercises that will be about writing XPaths and RegEx rules. For this purpose, we will use some open source tools.

One of the best open source platforms for practising writing RegEx rules is `https://regex101.com/`:

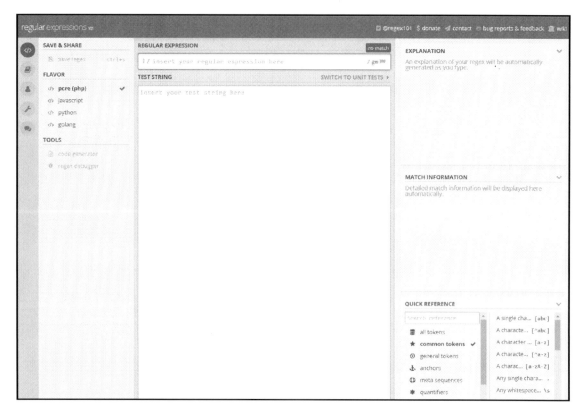

Regular expressions on regex101.com

As you see from the screenshot of `regex101.com`, the following is true:

- You can add some text strings to the **Test String** part and you can add your regular expressions to the **Regular Expression** part.
- On the **Test String** part, you will be able to see the matched strings.

- For testing your XPath rules, you can use Google Chrome's developer tools.
- You can reach this menu through the **More Tools** section; click on those three dots on your Chrome browser, as shown in the following screenshot:

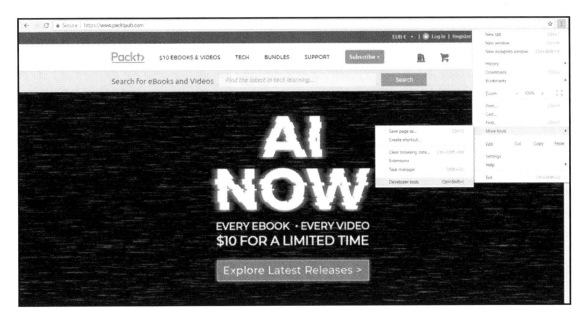

Developer tools option on the web page

- When you click **Developer tools**, you will be able to see following screen:

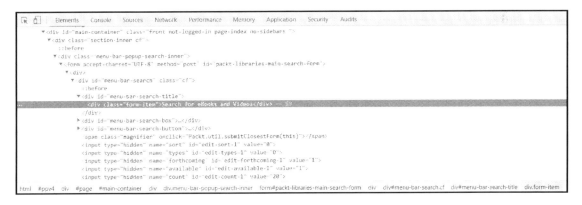

Google Chrome Developer tools

RegEx exercises

In this part, we are going to focus on hands-on exercises about RegEx rules. We will start by matching email addresses on a given text:

- Let's assume that we have text such as the following, and we would like to catch these email addresses:
    - Olgun Aydin, info@olgunaydin.com, Gdansk, Poland
    - Olgun Aydin, olgunaydinn@gmail.com, Gdansk, Poland
    - Olgun Aydin, olgun.aydin@olgunaydin.com, Gdansk, Poland
- Let's think about this problem. Email addresses have lowercase letters and can have some special characters such as dots
- The pattern looks like this: [some letters] OR [some letters, '.', some letters] @ [some letters] ["."] [some letters]
- We can write our regex rule as follows: (([a-z]+)|([a-z]+\.[a-z]+))@[a-z]+\.[a-z]+

Let's see how to use regex101.com. For this example, you can put your text to the text strings part, and you can write your regex rule to the regex string part.

As you see that, this tool is really straightforward. It's easy to see matched characters with different colors. As it is seen in the following screen shot, the **Match Information** part also gives us information about matched characters and the meaning of colors on the **Explanation** part:

Testing RegEx rules on `regex101.com`

1. Let's assume that now we have text like following and we would like to catch the e-mail addresses. As you can see, some of them have numeric characters:

   - `Olgun Aydin, info1@olgunaydin.com, Gdansk, Poland`
   - `Olgun Aydin, olgunaydinn88@gmail.com, Gdansk, Poland`
   - `Olgun Aydin, olgun.aydin35@olgunaydin.com, Gdansk, Poland`

2. Let's think about this problem. Email addresses have lowercase letters, and numeric characters can also have some special characters such as dot

3. The pattern looks like this: `[some letters] [ some numbers] OR [some letters, '.', some letters] [ some numbers] @ [some letters] ["."] [some letters]`

4. Then we can write our regex rule as follows: `(([a-z]+[0-9]+)|([a-z]+\.[a-z]+[0-9]+))@[a-z]+\.[a-z]+`

You can also put your text to the text strings part, and you can write your regex rule to the regex string part. It will look as shown in the following screenshot:

Testing RegEx rules on regex101.com

XPath exercises

In this part, we are going to focus on hands-on exercises about XPath rules. We will start with matching some XML nodes and attributes on Packt's website. We will use the Google Chrome Developers Tool.

Let's get started:

1. Navigate to Packt's web site and open Google Chrome's Developers Tool.
2. When you open this tool, you will see the following screen:

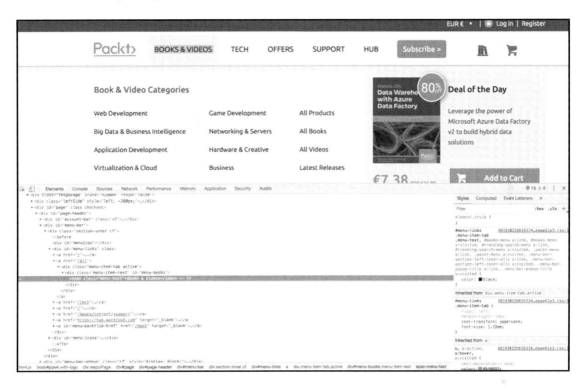

Google Chrome Developer tools

3. To write XPath rules, the console should be used, and the XPath rules should be written as shown: `$x('//*[@id="menu-books"]')`.

4. If we run this XPath rule, we will get the results shown in the following screenshot:

```
> $x('//*[@id="menu-books"]')
< ▼ [div#menu-books.menu-item-text] 🔘
    ▼ 0: div#menu-books.menu-item-text
        accessKey: ""
        align: ""
        assignedSlot: null
      ▶ attributeStyleMap: StylePropertyMap {size: 0}
      ▶ attributes: NamedNodeMap {0: class, 1: id, class: class, id: id, length: 2}
        autocapitalize: ""
        baseURI: "https://www.packtpub.com/"
        childElementCount: 1
      ▶ childNodes: NodeList(3) [text, span.menu-text, text]
      ▶ children: HTMLCollection [span.menu-text]
      ▶ classList: DOMTokenList ["menu-item-text", value: "menu-item-text"]
        className: "menu-item-text"
        clientHeight: 65
        clientLeft: 0
        clientTop: 0
        clientWidth: 156
        contentEditable: "inherit"
      ▶ dataset: DOMStringMap {}
        dir: ""
        draggable: false
      ▶ firstChild: text
      ▶ firstElementChild: span.menu-text
        hidden: false
```

Elements listed related to the XPath rule

Let's start to write some XPath rules from the scratch:

1. Let's assume that we would like to get the menu title on the top of the landing page of the Packt's website.
2. If you right-click and click on **Inspect Element** on the top of the landing page, you will see the the following XML structure:

HTML structure after clicking Inspect Element

Our task is collecting texts on the top of the landing page of the Packt's web page. For this purpose, we are going to write the following XPath rule:

- Texts at the top are under the class attribute that is named `menu-item-text` of `div`.
- Using two back slashes is always advantageous. It means "Catch any `div` classes". Thanks to this, you don't need to define the exact path of the related `div` element (`//div[@class="menu-item-text"]/span/text()`).

Results will be as shown in the following screenshot. It's clearly seen that, since we didn't mention specific text, we got all of the texts. If we want to have specific text, we should have specified which text:

```
>  $x('//div[@class="menu-item-text"]/span/text()')
<  ▼(18) [text, text, text, text, text, text, text, text, text, text, text, text, text, text, text, text, text, text] ◉
      ▶ 0: text
      ▶ 1: text
      ▶ 2: text
      ▶ 3: text
      ▶ 4: text
      ▶ 5: text
      ▶ 6: text
      ▶ 7: text
      ▶ 8: text
      ▶ 9: text
      ▶ 10: text
      ▶ 11: text
      ▶ 12: text
      ▶ 13: text
      ▶ 14: text
      ▶ 15: text
      ▶ 16: text
      ▶ 17: text
        length: 18
      ▶ __proto__: Array(0)
```

Elements listed related to the XPath rule

If we would like to have, let's say, the first text on the path, the XPath rule should be as shown next, and we should be more specific. Because we used class attributes to define the path, there are some other nodes that also have a class attribute named `menu-item-text`:

- If we want to get the first text on the menu, which is **BOOKS&VIDEOS**, we should use the ID attribute of the div element. XPath should be as shown follows: `//div[@id="menu-books"]/span/text()`

The results are shown in following screenshot. It's clearly seen that we have managed to get the text about the first text on the menu:

```
>   $x('//div[@id="menu-books"]/span/text()')
<   ▼ [text] 🔢
      ▼ 0: text
          assignedSlot: null
          baseURI: "https://www.packtpub.com/"
        ▶ childNodes: NodeList []
          data: "Books & Videos"
          firstChild: null
          isConnected: true
          lastChild: null
          length: 14
          nextElementSibling: null
          nextSibling: null
          nodeName: "#text"
          nodeType: 3
          nodeValue: "Books & Videos"
        ▶ ownerDocument: document
        ▶ parentElement: span.menu-text
        ▶ parentNode: span.menu-text
          previousElementSibling: null
          previousSibling: null
          textContent: "Books & Videos"
          wholeText: "Books & Videos"
        ▶ __proto__: Text
      length: 1
      ▶ __proto__: Array(0)
```

Elements listed related to the XPath rule

Summary

In this chapter, we have tried to focus on the idea behind XPath and RegEx; we became familiar with tools to write/test RegEx and XPath rules. In the exercise section, we focused on a real-life example and tried to write RegEx and XPath rules by using the tools that were mentioned.

In the next chapter, we will talk about the `rvest` library of R. We will investigate how it works and how to build scraping systems using the `rvest` library.

3
Web Scraping with rvest

All the data we need today is already available on the internet, which is great news for data scientists. The only barrier to using this data is the ability to access it. There are some platforms that even include APIs (such as Twitter) that support data collection from web pages, but it is not possible to crawl most web pages using this advantage.

Before we go on to scrape the web with R, we need to specify that this is advanced data analysis, data collection. We will use the **Hadley Wickham's method** for web scraping using rvest. The package also requires `selectr` and `xml2` packages.

The way to operate the rvest pole is simple and straightforward. Just as we first made web pages manually, the rvest package defines the web page link as the first step. After that, appropriate labels have to be defined. The HTML language edits content using various tags and selectors. These selectors must be identified and marked for storage of their contents by the harvest package. Then, all the engraved data can be transformed into an appropriate dataset, and analysis can be performed.

In this section, we will discuss in detail how fast and practical it is to use R for web scraping. After this section, you will gain expertise in using R to collect data over the internet.

The topics to be covered in this chapter are as follows:

- Introducing rvest
- Step-by-step web scraping with rvest

Introducing rvest

Most of the data on the web is in large scale as HTML. It is often not available in a form that is useful for analysis, such as hierarchical or tree-based:

```html
<html>
 <head>
 <title>Looks like a tittle</title>
 </head>
 <body>
 <p align="center">What's up ?</p>
 </body>
</html>
```

rvest is a very useful R library that helps you collect information from web pages. It is designed to work with magrittr, inspired by libraries such as BeatifulSoup.

To start the web scraping process, you first need to master the R bases. In this section, we will perform web scraping step by step, using the rvest R package written by Hadley Wickham.

 For more information about the rvesr package, visit the following URLs.CRAN Page: `https://cran.r-project.org/web/packages/rvest/index.html` rvest on github: `https://github.com/hadley/rvest`.

 Make sure this package is installed. If you do not have this package right now, you can use the following code to install it: `install.packages('rvest')`.

Let's take a look at some important functions in rvest:

Function	Description
read_html()	Create an html document from a URL, a file on a disk, or a string containing HTML.
html_nodes(doc, "table td")	Select parts of a document using css selectors.
html_nodes(doc, xpath = "//table//td")	Select parts of a document using xpath selectors.
html_tag()	Extract components with the name of the tag.
html_text()	Extract text from html document.
html_attr()	Get a single html attribute.
html_attrs()	Get all HTML attributes.
xml()	Working with XML files.
xml_node()	Extract XML components.
html_table()	Parse HTML tables into a data frame.
html_form() set_values() submit_form()	Extract, modify, and submit forms.
guess_encoding(), repair_encoding()	Detect and repair problems regarding encoding.

Step-by-step web scraping with rvest

After talking about the fundamentals of the rvest library, now we are going to deep dive into web scraping with rvest. We are going to talk about how to collect URLs from the website we would like to scrape.

We will use some simple regex rules for this issue. As we have learned how XPath works, then its time to write XPath rules. Once we have XPath rules and regex rules ready, we will jump into writing scripts to collect data from the website. That would be great, if we have a chance to play with the data we are going to collect. Don't worry; we will play with data, draw some plots, and create some charts.

We will collect a dataset from a blog, which is about big data (www.devveri.com). This website provides useful information about big data, data science domains. It is totally free of charge. People can visit this website and find use cases, exercises, and discussions regarding big-data technologies.

Let's start collecting information to find out how many articles there are in each category. You can find this information on the main page of the blog, using the following URL: `http://devveri.com/`. The screenshot shown is about the main page of the blog.

- As you see on the left-hand side, there are articles that were published recently. On the right-hand side, you can see categories and article counts of each categories:

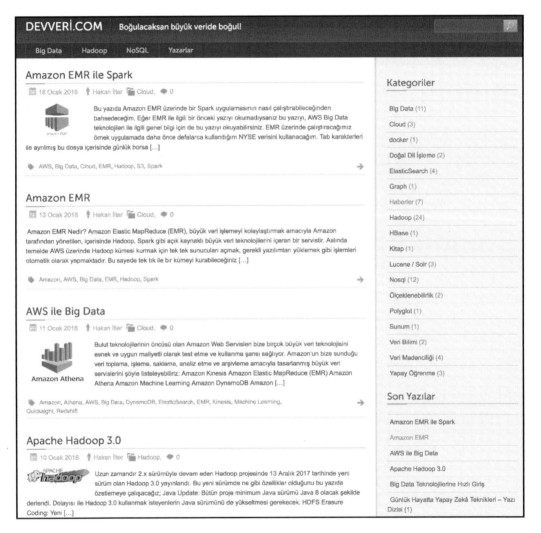

Landing page of devveri.com

- To collect the information about how many articles we have for each categories, we will use the landing page URL of the website. We will be interested in the right-hand side of the web page shown in the following image:

Categories on the landing page

- The following codes could be used to load the library and store the URL to the variable:

```
library(rvest)

urls <- "http://devveri.com/"
```

- If we print the URLs variable, it will look like the following image on the R Studio:

R Output

Now let's talk about the comment counts of the articles. Because this web page is about sharing useful information about recent technologies regarding current development in the big-data and data science domain, readers can easily ask questions to the author or discuss about the article with other readers easily just by commenting to articles.

Also, it's easy to see comment counts for each article on the category page. You can see one of the articles that was already commented on by readers in following screenshot. As you see, this article was commented on three times:

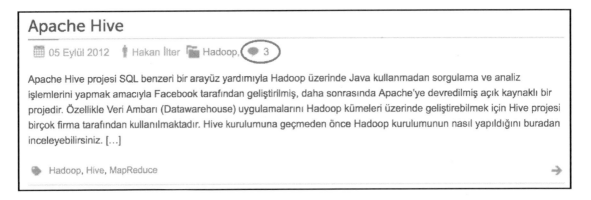

Article preview

In following part, we will also write XPath rules to collect this information, and then will be writing R script to collect the information, and at final step we will play with data to create some charts and plots.

Writing XPath rules

In this part, we are going to create our XPath rules to parse the HTML document we will collect:

- First of all, we will write XPath rules to collect information from the left-hand side of the web page, in other words, to collect information about how many articles there are for each categories.
- Let's navigate the landing page of the website `devveri.com`. As we exercised in previous chapter, will use Google Developer Tools to create and test XPath rules.
- To use **Google Developer Tools**, we can right-click on an element, which we are interested in extracting data from.
- Click **Inspect Element**. On the following screenshot, we marked the elements regarding categories:

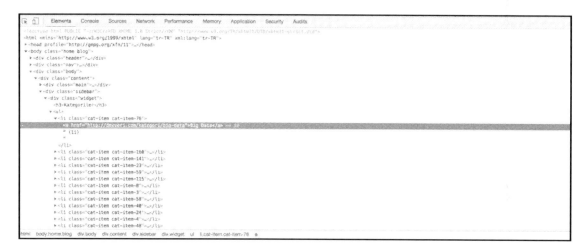

Inspecting element using Google Developer Tools

- Let's write XPath rules to get the categories. We are looking for the information about how many article there are for each categories and the name of the categories:

```
$x('/html/body/div[3]/div/div[2]/div[1]/ul/li/a/text()')
```

- If you type the XPath rule to the console on the Developer Tools, you will get the following elements. As you can see, we have eighteen text elements, because there are eighteen categories shown on the left-hand side of the page:

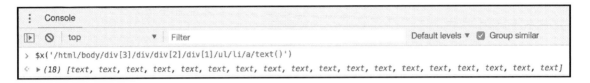

Wiev from console of Google Developer Tools

- Let's open a text element and see how it looks. As you see, we managed to get the text content, which we are interested in.

In the next part, we will experience how to manage to extract this information with R. As you can see from the wholeText section, we only have category names:

```
>  $x('/html/body/div[3]/div/div[2]/div[1]/ul/li[2]/a/text()')
<  ▼ [text] ℹ
      ▼ 0: text
          assignedSlot: null
          baseURI: "http://devveri.com/"
        ▶ childNodes: NodeList []
          data: "Cloud"
          firstChild: null
          isConnected: true
          lastChild: null
          length: 5
          nextElementSibling: null
          nextSibling: null
          nodeName: "#text"
          nodeType: 3
          nodeValue: "Cloud"
        ▶ ownerDocument: document
        ▶ parentElement: a
        ▶ parentNode: a
          previousElementSibling: null
          previousSibling: null
          textContent: "Cloud"
          wholeText: "Cloud"
        ▶ __proto__: Text
        length: 1
      ▶ __proto__: Array(0)
```

Still, we will need to collect article counts for each categories:

- Use the following XPath rule; it will help to collect this information from the web page.

```
$x('/html/body/div[3]/div/div[2]/div[1]/ul/li/text()')
```

- If you type the XPath rule to the console on the Developer Tools, you will get the following elements.

As you can see, we have 18 text elements, because there are eighteen categories shown on the left-hand side of the page:

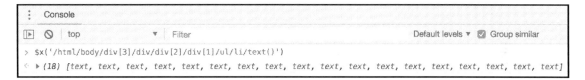

Now it's time to start collecting URLs for articles. Because, at this stage, we are going to collect comment counts for articles that were written recently. For this issue, it would be good to have the article name and the date of the articles. If we write the name of the first article, we will get the element regarding the name of the article, as shown in the following screenshot:

Element of the name of article

- Let's write XPath rules to get the name of the article. We are looking for the name of the article:

```
$x('/html/body/div[3]/div/div[1]/div/h2/a/text()')
```

- If you type the XPath rule to the Developer Tools console, you will get the following elements. As you can see, we have 15 text elements, because there are 15 article previews on this page:

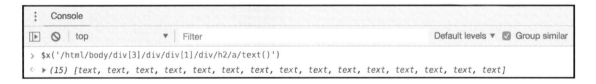

- Let's open the first text element and see how it looks. As you see, we managed to get the text content that we are interested in.

In the next part, we will experience how to extract this information with R:

```
⋮  Console
▶ ⊘   top                    ▼ | Filter                          Default levels ▼  ☑ Group similar
>  $x('/html/body/div[3]/div/div[1]/div/h2/a/text()')
‹  ▼ (15) [text, text, text, text, text, text, text, text, text, text, text, text, text, text, text] ▣
     ▼ 0: text
         assignedSlot: null
         baseURI: "http://devveri.com/"
       ▶ childNodes: NodeList []
         data: "Amazon EMR ile Spark"
         firstChild: null
         isConnected: true
         lastChild: null
         length: 20
         nextElementSibling: null
         nextSibling: null
         nodeName: "#text"
         nodeType: 3
         nodeValue: "Amazon EMR ile Spark"
       ▶ ownerDocument: document
       ▶ parentElement: a
       ▶ parentNode: a
         previousElementSibling: null
         previousSibling: null
         textContent: "Amazon EMR ile Spark"
         wholeText: "Amazon EMR ile Spark"
       ▶ __proto__: Text
```

We have the names of the articles, as we decided we should also collect the date and comment counts of the articles:

- The following XPath rule will help us to collect created date of the articles in text format:

  ```
  $x('/html/body/div[3]/div/div[1]/div/p[1]/span[1]/text()')
  ```

- If you type the XPath rule on the Developer Tools console, you will get the elements, as shown in the following screenshot:

As you can see, we have 15 text elements regarding dates, because there are 15 article previews on this page:

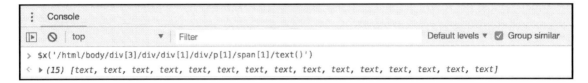

- Let's open the first text element and see how it looks.

As you can see, we managed to get the text content that we are interested in. In the next part, we will experience how to extract this information with R:

We have the names of the articles and have created dates of the articles. As we decided, we should still collect the comment counts of the articles:

- The following XPath rule will help us to collect comment counts:

```
$x('/html/body/div[3]/div/div[1]/div/p[1]/span[4]/a/text()')
```

- If you type the XPath rule to the Developer Tools console, you will get the elements, as shown in the following screenshot.

As you can see, we have 15 text elements regarding comment counts, because there are fifteen article previews on this page:

```
⋮   Console

▶  ⃠  top              ▼  Filter                              Default levels ▼  ✓ Group similar

> $x('/html/body/div[3]/div/div[1]/div/p[1]/span[4]/a/text()')
< ▶ (15) [text, text, text, text, text, text, text, text, text, text, text, text, text, text, text]
```

- Let's open the first text element and see how it looks.

You see, we managed to get the text content that we are interested in. In the next part, we will experience how to extract this information with R:

```
⋮   Console

▶  ⃠  top              ▼  Filter                              Default levels ▼  ✓ Group similar

> $x('/html/body/div[3]/div/div[1]/div/p[1]/span[4]/a/text()')
< ▼ (15) [text, text, text, text, text, text, text, text, text, text, text, text, text, text, text]
    ▼ 0: text
        assignedSlot: null
        baseURI: "http://devveri.com/"
      ▶ childNodes: NodeList []
        data: "0"
        firstChild: null
        isConnected: true
        lastChild: null
        length: 1
        nextElementSibling: null
        nextSibling: null
        nodeName: "#text"
        nodeType: 3
        nodeValue: "0"
      ▶ ownerDocument: document
      ▶ parentElement: a
      ▶ parentNode: a
        previousElementSibling: null
        previousSibling: null
        textContent: "0"
        wholeText: "0"
      ▶ __proto__: Text
```

Writing your first scraping script

Let's start to write our first scraping using R. In previous sections, we have already created XPath rules and URLs that we are interested in. We will start by collecting category counts and information about how many articles there are for each article:

- First of all, we have called an rvest library using the library function. We should load the rvest library using the following command:

```
library(rvest)
```

- Now we need to create NULL variables, because we are going to save count of articles for each categories and the name of the categories.
- For this purpose, we are creating category and count variables:

```
#creating NULL variables
category<- NULL
count <- NULL
```

- Now it's time to create a variable that includes the URL that we would like to navigate and collect data.
- As we mentioned in the previous section, we would like to collect data from first page of the website. By using the following code block, we are assigning a URL to the URLs variable:

```
#links for page
urls <- "http://devveri.com/"
```

Now for the most exciting part: Collecting data!

The following script is first of all visit the URL of the web page, collecting HTML nodes using the read_html function. To parse HTML nodes, we are using XPath rules that we have already created in the previous section. For this issue, we are using the html_nodes function, and we are defining our XPath rules ,which we already have, inside the function:

```
library(rvest)

#creating NULL variables
category<- NULL
count <- NULL

#links for page
urls <- "http://devveri.com/"
```

```
#reading main url
h <- read_html(urls)
#getting categories
c<- html_nodes(h, xpath =
'/html/body/div[3]/div/div[2]/div[1]/ul/li/a/text()')
#getting counts
cc<- html_nodes(h, xpath =
'/html/body/div[3]/div/div[2]/div[1]/ul/li/text()')
#saving results, converting XMLs to character
category<- as.matrix(as.character(c))
count<- as.matrix(as.character(cc))
```

- We can use the `data.frame` function to see categories and counts together.
- You will get the following result on R, when you run the script on the first line as shown in the following code block:

```
> data.frame(category,count)
          category count
1  Big Data (11)\n
2  Cloud (3)\n
3  docker (1)\n
4  Doğal Dil İşleme (2)\n
5  ElasticSearch (4)\n
6  Graph (1)\n
7  Haberler (7)\n
8  Hadoop (24)\n
9  HBase (1)\n
10 Kitap (1)\n
11 Lucene / Solr (3)\n
12 Nosql (12)\n
13 Ölçeklenebilirlik (2)\n
14 Polyglot (1)\n
15 Sunum (1)\n
16 Veri Bilimi (2)\n
17 Veri Madenciliği (4)\n
18 Yapay Öğrenme (3)\n
```

- Now it's time to collect the name, comment counts, and the date of the articles that we wrote recently.
- We have called the rvest library using the library function and should load the rvest library using the following command:

```
library(rvest)
```

- Now we need to create the NULL variable. Because we are going to save the comment counts, the date, and the name of the articles, we are creating the name, date, and comment_count variables:

```
#creating NULL variables
name <- NULL
date <- NULL
comment_count <- NULL
```

The following script is first of all visit the URL of the web page, collecting HTML nodes using the
read_html function. To parse HTML nodes, we are using XPath rules that we have already created in the previous section. For this issue, we are using the html_nodes function, and we are defining our XPath rules, which we already have, inside the function:

```
#creating NULL variables
name <- NULL
date <- NULL
comment_count <- NULL

#links for page
urls <- "http://devveri.com/"

#reading main url
h <- read_html(urls)

#getting names
n<- html_nodes(h, xpath = '/html/body/div[3]/div/div[1]/div/h2/a/text()')

#getting dates
d<- html_nodes(h, xpath =
'/html/body/div[3]/div/div[1]/div/p[1]/span[1]/text()')

#getting comment counts
comc<- html_nodes(h, xpath =
'/html/body/div[3]/div/div[1]/div/p[1]/span[4]/a/text()')

#saving results
name<- as.matrix(as.character(n))
date<- as.matrix(as.character(d))
comment_count<- as.matrix(as.character(comc))
```

We managed to collect the name, comment counts, and the date of the articles:

- We can use the data.frame function to see the name, date, and comment counts variables together:

```
> data.frame(name,date,comment_count)
  name date comment_count
1 Amazon EMR ile Spark 18 Ocak 2018 0
2 Amazon EMR 13 Ocak 2018 0
3 AWS ile Big Data 11 Ocak 2018 0
4 Apache Hadoop 3.0 10 Ocak 2018 0
5 Big Data Teknolojilerine Hızlı Giriş 19 Haziran 2017 1
6 Günlük Hayatta Yapay Zekâ Teknikleri — Yazı Dizisi (1) 29 Mart
  2016 0
7 Hive Veritabanları Arası Tablo Taşıma 18 Şubat 2016 0
8 Basit Lineer Regresyon 11 Şubat 2016 2
9 Apache Sentry ile Yetkilendirme 10 Ocak 2016 0
10 Hive İç İçe Sorgu Kullanımı 09 Aralık 2015 2
11 Kmeans ve Kmedoids Kümeleme 07 Aralık 2015 0
12 Veri analizinde yeni alışkanlıklar 25 Kasım 2015 0
13 Daha İyi Bir Veri Bilimcisi Olmanız İçin 5 İnanılmaz Yol 02
Kasım 2015 1
14 R ile Korelasyon, Regresyon ve Zaman Serisi Analizleri 12 Ekim
2015 3
15 Data Driven Kavramı ve II. Faz 28 Eylül 2015 0
```

Playing with data

We have two different datasets. We already have collected categories and article counts for each categories, and we have already collected the name, date, and comment counts articles, which were written recently.

Let's start by playing data regarding categories and the article counts for each category:

- We should implement basic text manipulation methods to have counts in a more proper format. Because counts look as shown here, we have to apply basic text to get rid of the characters:

```
> count
      [,1]
[1,]  " (11)\n"
[2,]  " (3)\n"
[3,]  " (1)\n"
[4,]  " (2)\n"
[5,]  " (4)\n"
[6,]  " (1)\n"
[7,]  " (7)\n"
[8,]  " (24)\n"
[9,]  " (1)\n"
[10,]  " (1)\n"
[11,]  " (3)\n"
```

```
[12,]  "  (12) \n"
[13,]  "   (2) \n"
[14,]  "   (1) \n"
[15,]  "   (1) \n"
[16,]  "   (2) \n"
[17,]  "   (4) \n"
[18,]  "   (3) \n"
```

- We should be replacing "\n", "(" and ")" with "". For this issue, we are going to use the `str_replace_all` function. To use the `str_replace_all` function, we need to install the `stringr` package and load it:

```
count <- str_replace_all(count,"\\(","")
count <- str_replace_all(count,"\\)","")
count <- str_replace_all(count,"\n","")
```

- Now we have article counts in a better format. If we create the data frame using the new version of the count variable and article categories, we will have following result:

```
> data.frame(category,count)
   category count
1  Big Data 11
2  Cloud 3
3  docker 1
4  Doğal Dil İşleme 2
5  ElasticSearch 4
6  Graph 1
7  Haberler 7
8  Hadoop 24
9  HBase 1
10 Kitap 1
11 Lucene / Solr 3
12 Nosql 12
13 Ölçeklenebilirlik 2
14 Polyglot 1
15 Sunum 1
16 Veri Bilimi 2
17 Veri Madenciliği 4
18 Yapay Öğrenme 3
```

- Let's assign this data frame to variable and cast the count as numeric, because they are in string format. If we run the following code, we will create a new data frame and convert counts as numeric:

```
categories <- data.frame(category,count)
categories$count<-as.numeric(categories$count)
```

Now we are ready to create some charts:

- To do this, we can use interactive plotting library of R, `plotly`, if you don't already have it installed on your R environment.
- You can install it using the `install.packages("plotly")` command.
- Then, of course, we have to call this library using the `library(plotly)` command:

```
plot_ly(categories, x = ~category, y = ~count, type = 'bar')
```

The following command will help us to create a bar chart to show article counts for each category:

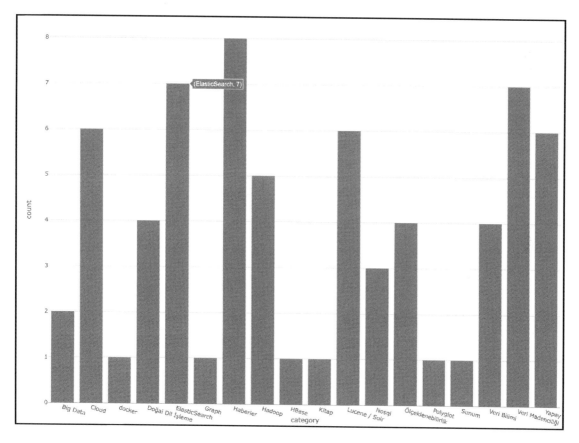

Bar chart for each category

- We can create some charts using our second dataset that is about the date, name, and comment counts of articles that were written recently.

As you remember, we already collected the following data for this purpose:

```
> data.frame(name,date,comment_count)
  name date comment_count
1 Amazon EMR ile Spark 18 Ocak 2018 0
2 Amazon EMR 13 Ocak 2018 0
3 AWS ile Big Data 11 Ocak 2018 0
.
.
.
```

We are ready to create our final data frame. But, don't forget, comment counts are still in string format:

- We have to cast them to numeric format. For this purpose, we can use the `as.numeric` function:

```
comments<- data.frame(name,date,comment_count)
comments$comment_count<- as.numeric(comments$comment_count)
```

Now we're ready to go! Calcuate the comment counts per date:

- To do this, we can use `aggregate` function:

```
avg_comment_counts <- aggregate(comment_count~date, data = comments, FUN= "mean")
```

- Now we have daily average comment counts, let's create a line chart to see the daily average ratings changes:

```
plot(avg_comment_counts,type = "l")
```

The following line chart shows us the average comment counts based on dates:

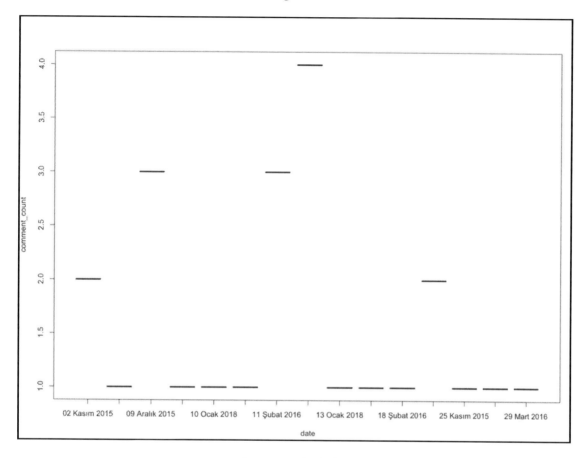

Average comments based on dates

- Now, let's investigate more about the dataset. Seeing the summary statistics of the comment counts would be really good.
- In this part, we are going to calculate the minimum, maximum, mean, and median value of the comment counts and then create bar chart that shows those summary statistics.
- By using the following commands, we are going to calculate those summary statistics:

```
min_comment_count<- min(comments$comment_count)
max_comment_count<- max(comments$comment_count)
avg_comment_count<- mean(comments$comment_count)
median_comment_count<- median(comments$comment_count)
```

- Let's create a dataframe that contains the metrics calculated:

```
summary<- data.frame(min_comment_count, max_comment_count,
avg_comment_count, median_comment_count)
```

Now we have summary statistics, we can create a bar chart using those values by using the following commands. Because on our plot there will be more than one different category, we are going to use the add_trace function:

```
plot_ly(x = "min", y = summary$min_comment_count, type = 'bar',name='min')
%>%
 add_trace(x = "max", y = summary$max_comment_count, type =
'bar',name='max')%>%
 add_trace(x = "avg", y = summary$avg_comment_count, type =
'bar',name='average')%>%
 add_trace(x = "median", y = summary$median_comment_count, type =
'bar',name='median')
```

As you can see, this bar chart is a summary of the statistics of the daily average of the ratings:

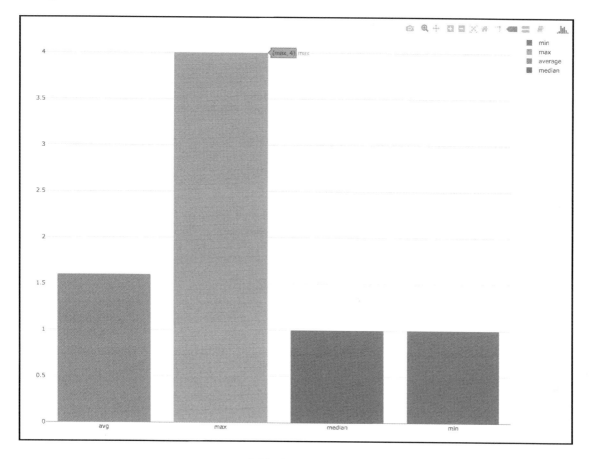

Statistics of daily average rating

Summary

In this chapter, we have learned how to write a scraping script using the rvest library. First, we worked on how to collect URLs, and then we worked on how to create XPath rules. After that, we wrote our first web scraping script using the rvest library. We have applied basic text and manipulation techniques. Once we had the final data ready, we calculated the daily average comment counts, and at the final step, we created a line plot using basic R plots and plotly plots to visualize the average comment count, article counts for each categories, and the summary statistics of the comment counts.

In the next chapter, we will talk about the fundamentals of Selenium and how to do web scraping using the RSelenium library. At the end of the next chapter, we will be writing R script to collect data from the web using Selenium.

4
Web Scraping with Rselenium

Selenium has been developed to test web applications. Selenium allows writing tests without the need to learn any test script language (Selenium IDE). In addition, C #, Groovy, Java, Perl, PHP, Python, Ruby and Scala, such as a series of popular programming language to provide testing environment. These tests can then be run on most modern web browsers. Selenium is an open source software under the Apache 2.0 license.

Selenium is designed to automate the operations of a web browser. With Selenium, any user can manually perform interactions that can be performed manually. Selenium can be used for any kind of automation, but the priority is to create automated web application tests.

The name of Selenium comes from a joke. Another automated testing framework was used as a popup during the development of Selenium, and the company was Mercury Interactive. Since Selenium is a well-known antidote to Mercury poisoning, this name has been suggested.

Selenium can be defined as an umbrella that encompasses a variety of tools and libraries that provide web browser automation. Selenium provides the infrastructure for the W3C WebDriver specification and provides a platform interface compatible with all major web browsers. The source code for Selenium is available with an Apache 2.0 license.

Selenium is intended for the automated testing of web applications, and it performs brilliantly as a general- purpose browser automation tool.

Selenium is a package designed to be used to test open source web applications for web applications for different browsers and platforms. The main purpose of Selenium is to automate web-based applications.

Web scraping is an important skill for data scientists. Each data set you want to analyze may not be available in a suitable format, and if you want to make unique analyzes, it is also important to make a decent data set by scraping yourself.

Static scraping is sufficient for retrieving data from static lists, but we need to automate the browser and interact with the DOM to retrieve data from a web site controlled by JavaScript, or to retrieve data from a parcel that is placed as an iframe item by JavaScript. One of the best tools for this purpose is Selenium

In this chapter, we will learn about the following topics:

- The advantages and disadvantages of using Selenium for web scraping
- RSelenium
- Step-by-step web scraping with RSelenium

Advantages and disadvantages of using Selenium for web scraping

Because WebDriver uses a real web browser to access the web site, there is no difference than browsing the web by a human. When you navigate to a web page using WebDriver, the browser loads all the website resources (JavaScript files, images, css files, and so on) and executes all the JavaScripts on the page. It also keeps all cookies created by your websites. This makes it very difficult to determine whether a real person or a robot has accessed the website. With WebDriver, this can be done in a few simple steps, although it's really hard to simulate all these actions in a program that sends *handmade* HTTP requests to the server.

Sometimes, the data to be extracted may not be included in the raw HTML that was received after an HTTP request was made. Although it is possible to receive this data only with HTTP requests, it is usually easier to allow a web browser to do it for you. In these situations, WebDriver is a great help.

You need a web browser to see how the structure and content of the web page looks. Using WebDriver is a great way to get screenshots while surfing the web.

Even if you need to scrape a small portion of a website, it is important that your program is associated with all the Selenium WebDriver poles and that the WebDriver driver can be installed on each browser.

When a web page is scraped using WebDriver, the entire web browser is loaded into the system memory. This takes a long time and consumes the system resources, and may cause the security systems to react.

Web browsers will wait until the entire web page is loaded and will only allow you to access the website's assets. Scraping can take longer than sending simple HTTP requests to a web server.

Web browsers load additional files such as css, js, and image files when navigating a web page.

When we do a lot of web scraping using WebDriver, this can easily be detected by any JavaScript-based trafficking tool such as Google Analytics.

RSelenium

RSelenium is designed to make it easy to connect to a Selenium server or a remote Selenium server. RSelenium allows connection from the R environment to the Selenium Webdriver API. Selenium is a project that focuses on automating web browsers.

Selenium Server is an independent java program that allows you to run HTML test suites in different browsers.

If you want to navigate your website using a browser on the same machine that RSelenium is running on, you need to run Selenium Server on that machine.

RSelenium is one of the most useful poles of R. With just a few lines of code, you can automate web pages and create scraping systems. This is useful for testing web applications as well as for collecting data from multiple web pages.

If you are not familiar with this R library, it will be useful to read the guide created for beginners.

RSelenium is an R library that allows you to use the Selenium 2.0 WebDriver project, designed to automatically test Web applications, in the R environment.

To use Selenium in R, you need to have R language loaded on your system. Using R Studio IDE is highly recommended. To download the RSelenium package, you can use following command `install_github("ropensci/RSelenium")` and then you can load it into your current R session with `library("RSelenium")`.

More information about RSelenium can be found here:

- Github: `https://github.com/ropensci/RSelenium`
- rOpenSci: `https://ropensci.github.io/RSelenium/`

Step-by-step web scraping with RSelenium

In this part, we are going to focus on collecting data from Instagram by using RSelenium. First of all, we are going to navigate the URL of the Instagram post, and collects comments and parses comments to detect users who put comments and users who are mentioned.

Collecting data with RSelenium

Let's start collecting data from Instagram by using the `RSelenium` library. First of all, we have to load the `RSelenium` library using the following command:

```
#loading libraries
library(RSelenium)
```

Now we load Selenium drivers and start Selenium. It may take time, so please wait till loading finishes:

```
#loading drivers and starting selenium
rD <- rsDriver()
remDr <- rD[["client"]]
```

During loading drivers, you will see the following output on your RStudio console:

```
* DONE (RSelenium)
Warning message:
In strptime(x, fmt, tz = "GMT") :
  unknown timezone 'zone/tz/2018e.1.0/zoneinfo/Europe/Warsaw'
> library("RSelenium")
> rD <- rsDriver()
checking Selenium Server versions:
BEGIN: PREDOWNLOAD
BEGIN: DOWNLOAD
Creating directory: /Users/olgunaydin/Library/Application Support/b...
Downloading binary: https://www.googleapis.com/download/storage/v1/...

Creating directory: /Users/olgunaydin/Library/Application Support/b...
Downloading binary: https://www.googleapis.com/download/storage/v1/...

Creating directory: /Users/olgunaydin/Library/Application Support/b...
Downloading binary: https://www.googleapis.com/download/storage/v1/...
```

Loading Selenium Server

Let's navigate an Instagram post that has a `packtpub` hashtag:

```
#navigate post which has packtpub hashtag
remDr$navigate("https://www.instagram.com/p/BiFW2XFD8CM/?hl=en&tagged=packt
pub")
```

After running the following command, Selenium driver will start the Chrome browser, as shown in the following screenshot. As you can see, there is information that says, *Chrome is being controlled by automated test software*:

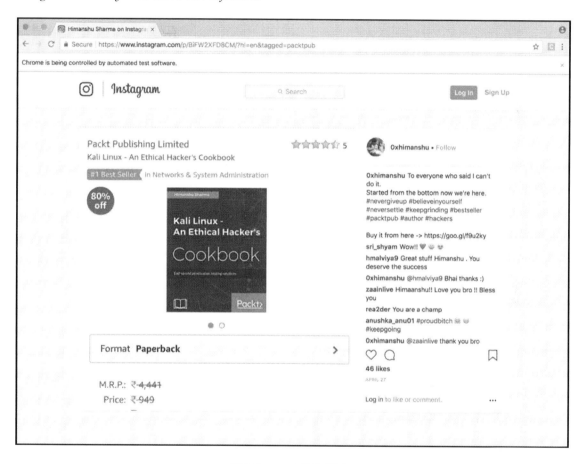

Chrome browser controlled by Selenium

Let's start to collect users who put comments and the users who were mentioned. First, we will start with collecting users who put comments to this post.

We are going to find HTML element that we are interested in. To do this, we are going to use the XPath rule. The XPath rule for getting the name of the user who commented will be as shown in the following code block:

```
$x('//*[@id="react-
root"]/section/main/div/div/article/div[2]/div[1]/ul/li[2]/div/div/div/a')
```

To find the HTML element, we should use the `findElement` object of `remDr`, so we can find the HTML element using the following command:

```
webElem2 <- remDr$findElement(using = "xpath",paste('//*[@id="react-
root"]/section/main/div/div/article/div[2]/div[1]/ul/li[2]/div/div/div/a',s
ep=""))
```

After finding the element we are interested in, we can use the `getElementText` object of `WebElem2`. We can use the following command to get the text element of the HTML element. As you can see, we managed to get the name of the user who commented to the post:

```
> webElem2$getElementText()[[1]][1]
[1] "sri_shyam"
```

Let's create the null variables that will be used for storing the names of the users who put comments:

```
username_mentioned_df<- NULL
```

Because we have nine comments for this post, we are going to use nine steps `for` loop. Not to be blocked by Instagram, we are putting a delay by using the `Sys.sleep` function:

```
for(j in 1:9)
{
 webElem2 <- remDr$findElement(using = "xpath",paste("//*[@id='react-
root']/section/main/div/div/article/div[2]/div[1]/ul/li[",j,"]/div/div/div/
a",sep=""))
 Sys.sleep(1)
 username_mentioned<- webElem2$getElementText()[[1]][1]
 username_mentioned_df <- rbind(username_mentioned_df,username_mentioned)
}
```

If we print the `user_name_mentioned_df` data frame, we will be able to see the data frame that contains the names of the users who put comments to the post:

```
> username_mentioned_df
  [,1]
username_mentioned "0xhimanshu"
username_mentioned "sri_shyam"
username_mentioned "hmalviya9"
username_mentioned "0xhimanshu"
username_mentioned "zaainlive"
username_mentioned "rea2der"
username_mentioned "anushka_anu01"
username_mentioned "0xhimanshu"
username_mentioned "dhruv_2204"
```

Now let's collect the names of the users who were mentioned in the comments for the post.

We are going to find the HTML element that we are interested in. To do this, we are going to use the XPath rule. The XPath rule for getting the name of the users who were mentioned will be as shown in the following code block:

```
$x("//*[@id='react-
root']/section/main/div/div/article/div[2]/div[1]/ul/li[4]/div/div/div/span
/a[1]")
```

To find the HTML element, we should use the `findElement` object of `remDr`, so we can find the HTML element using the following command:

```
webElem2 <- remDr$findElement(using = "xpath",paste("//*[@id='react-
root']/section/main/div/div/article/div[2]/div[1]/ul/li[4]/div/div/div/span
/a[1]",sep=""))
```

After finding the element that we are interested in, we can use the `getElementText` object of `WebElem2`. We can use the following command to get the text element of the HTML element. As you can see, we managed to get the name of the user, who was mentioned in the comment:

```
> webElem2$getElementText()[[1]][1]
[1] "@hmalviya9"
```

Let's create the null variables that will be used for storing the names of the users who put comments:

```
mentioned_username_df<- NULL
```

Because we have nine comments for this post, we are going to use nine steps `for` loop. Not to be blocked by Instagram, we are putting a delay by using the `Sys.sleep` function:

```
for(j in 1:9)
{
 webElem2 <- remDr$findElement(using = "xpath",paste("//*[@id='react-
root']/section/main/div/div/article/div[2]/div[1]/ul/li[",j,"]/div/div/div/
span",sep=""))
 mentioned_username_check<- webElem2$getElementText()[[1]][1]

 #checking if there is a mention or not
 if(str_detect(mentioned_username_check,"@")==TRUE)
 {
 webElem2 <- remDr$findElement(using = "xpath",paste("//*[@id='react-
root']/section/main/div/div/article/div[2]/div[1]/ul/li[",j,"]/div/div/div/
span/a[1]",sep=""))
 mentioned_username<- webElem2$getElementText()[[1]][1]
 }else{
 mentioned_username<- ""
 }
 mentioned_username_df <- rbind(mentioned_username_df,mentioned_username)
 Sys.sleep(1)
}
```

If we print the `mentioned_user_name_df` data frame, we will be able to see the data frame that contains the names of the users who were mentioned in the comments to the post:

```
> mentioned_username_df
                       [,1]
mentioned_username ""
mentioned_username ""
mentioned_username ""
mentioned_username "@hmalviya9"
mentioned_username ""
mentioned_username ""
mentioned_username ""
mentioned_username "@zaainlive"
mentioned_username ""
```

As you can see from the output shown, if we don't have any mentions, we leave these rows empty. If we take a look at the following snapshot, we can see that only the eighth and fifth comments have mentions:

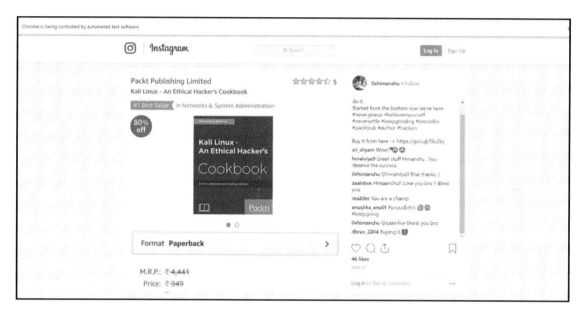

Chrome browser controlled by Selenium

Now let's try to trigger some events by using the RSelenium package. For example, we can click some buttons such as **Show more**, **Load more comments**, and so on.

As you remember, in `Chapter 3`, *Web Scraping with rvest*, we were dealing with collecting data from `Devveri.com` by using `rvest` library. Now we we are going to try to collect data from same web page by using RSelenium, also we will take a look at how to send click events using RSelenium.

First of all, we have to load the RSelenium library using following command:

```
#loading libraries
 library(RSelenium)
```

Now we are loading Selenium drivers and starting Selenium. It may take time, so please wait till loading finishes:

```
#loading drivers and starting selenium
rD <- rsDriver()
remDr <- rD[["client"]]
```

The Drivers will be loading on your RStudio console.

Let's navigate to the *tripadvisor* website, which has airline comments:

```
remDr$navigate("http://devveri.com/")
```

After running the command shown, Selenium Driver will start the Chrome browser, as shown in the following screenshot. As you can see, there is information that says, *Chrome is being controlled by automated test software*:

Chrome Browser controlled by Selenium

As you see from the preceding screenshot, we managed to navigate landing page of the web site. Now, let's try to open first article on this page using RSelenium. For this issue, first of all, we have to mark this part of the HTML using XPath and then we can send the click event to this web element:

```
webElem1 <- remDr$findElement(using = "xpath",
"/html/body/div[3]/div/div[1]/div[1]/h2/a")
```

When we run the preceding code, we will see the following page. As you see, we managed to open the first article:

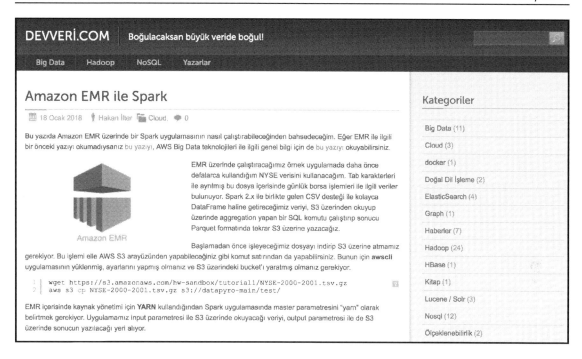

Chrome browser controlled by Selenium

Let's assume that we would like to visit similar articles, as you can see on the following screen shot which was taken from the bottom of the page, it's possible to navigate another article under this category:

Previous article in this category

Following command will help us to navigate previous article in this category:

```
webElem2 <- remDr$findElement(using = "xpath",
'//p[@class="pagination"]/span[@class="prev"]')
webElem2$clickElement()
```

If you run the the preceding code, you will see following page:

Navigating previous article

As long you run the following command, you get the previous articles in this category:

```
webElem2 <- remDr$findElement(using = "xpath",
'//p[@class="pagination"]/span[@class="prev"]')
webElem2$clickElement()
```

Now, let's practice using Regex rules. Sometimes, the data you collect from a website is not how you would like to see it. For example, let's try to see this more clearly by doing an exercise.

Let's assume that we are interested in collecting an email address as a contact information from a website. Let's navigate the contact page of `devveri.com`. Before navigating web page, it's better to stop Selenium Driver and start again. You can stop the server by using the following command. When you run `rD[["server"]]$stop()`, you will get a `TRUE` response after the server is closed:

```
> rD[["server"]]$stop()
[1]  TRUE
```

Now we can start the Selenium server again by using following command:

```
#loading drivers and starting selenium
 rD <- rsDriver()
 remDr <- rD[["client"]]
```

Let's navigate the landing page of the devveri.com :

```
remDr$navigate("http://devveri.com/")
```

After running the preceding command, Selenium Driver will start the Chrome browser, as shown in the following screenshot. As you can see, there is information that says, *Chrome is being controlled by automated test software*:

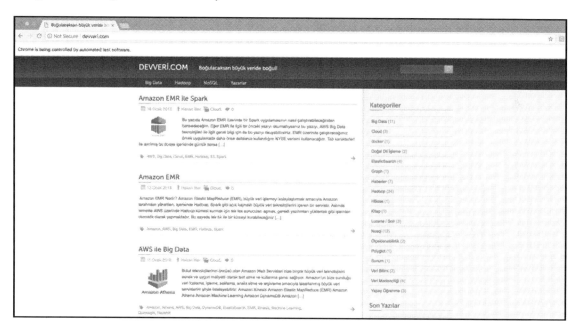

Chrome Browser controlled by Selenium

As you remember, on previous chapter we tried to collect category names and information about how many articles there are for each categories. For this issue, we used string replacement technique, now let's try to do it using RegEx rules. As you remember the part regarding categories is shown on the right hand side of the page

Kategoriler

Big Data (11)

Cloud (3)

docker (1)

Doğal Dil İşleme (2)

ElasticSearch (4)

Graph (1)

Haberler (7)

Hadoop (24)

HBase (1)

Kitap (1)

Lucene / Solr (3)

Nosql (12)

Ölçeklenebilirlik (2)

Polyglot (1)

Sunum (1)

Veri Bilimi (2)

Veri Madenciliği (4)

Yapay Öğrenme (3)

Categories on the landing page

Let's write XPath rules to get the categories. We are looking for the information about how many article there are for each categories and the name of the categories:

```
$x('/html/body/div[3]/div/div[2]/div[1]/ul/li/a/text()')
```

If you type the XPath rule to the on the **Developer Tools**, you will get the following elements. As you can see, we have eighteen text elements, because there are eighteen categories shown on the left-hand side of the page:

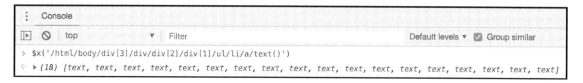

Wiev from console of Google Developer Tools

Using following command, we can collect category names and number of articles for the category:

```
webElem4 <- remDr$findElement(using = "xpath",
'/html/body/div[3]/div/div[2]/div[1]/ul/li')
webElem4$getElementText()
```

If you run the preceding code, you will get the following result.

```
> webElem4$getElementText()
[[1]]
[1] "Big Data (11)"
```

As you see, we have got the name of the category and number of articles for this category at the same time. We can parse this result and store name and number of articles in seperate variables. Following RegEx rule will help us to extract the information about number of articles:

```
[0-9][0-9]
```

Following RegEx rule will help us to extract the information about name of the category:

```
[a-zA-Z]+ [a-zA-Z]+
```

To apply RegEx rules in R, you can use `regexpr` function. First, we are going to assign the text, which includes information which we collected from the web page to a variable and define our RegEx rule, then use `regexpr` and `regmatches` functions. Let's first define assign the text which we collected from the web page to a variable and define our RegEx rule:

```
category<- webElem4$getElementText()[[1]][1]
regex_for_count<- regexpr("[0-9][0-9]",category)
```

Then we should use `regmatches` function to parse the text to get number of categories, using related RegEx rule:

```
count <- regmatches(category, regex_for_count)
```

If we print count variable, we will get following result. As you see we managed to get number of articles in the category:

```
count
[1] "11"
```

To get name of the category, we are going to use following commands:

```
regex_for_name<- regexpr("[a-zA-Z]+ [a-zA-Z]+",category)
```

If we use `regmatches` function to parse the text to get name of categories, using related RegEx rule:

```
name <-regmatches(category, regex_for_name)
```

If we print name variable, we will get following result. As you see we managed to get name of category:

```
> name
[1] "Big Data"
```

Summary

In this chapter, we have learned how to write scraping script using the RSelenium library. First, we worked on how to use selenium drivers on R and then we worked on how to use XPath rules with the RSelenium package. Afterward, we wrote our first web-scraping script using the RSelenium library to collect the user who commented to the specific post and who is mentioned in the comments to the specific post. Then we tried to send a click event and. Finally, we used Regex rules to extract the information that we were interested in.

In the next chapter, we will talk about the fundamentals of cron jobs and databases. At the end of the next chapter, we will be writing our creating cron job to schedule our web-scraping task and learn how to store collected data on databases.

5
Storing Data and Creating Cronjob

Cloud computing is a system of information technology that enables access to the configurable system resources at any time and can be accessed from anywhere, which can be quickly accessed with minimal administrative overhead on the internet. The cloud computing logic is based on the principle of sharing resources.

Instead of spending resources on computer infrastructure and the maintenance of institutions, cloud systems enable these resources to be broken down into basic businesses. Since the introduction of Amazon EC2 in 2006, the availability of high-capacity and high-speed networks, low-cost computers, and storage systems has been widespread. Hardware virtualization has also begun to be widely used.

In the 1960s, the first concepts of time sharing became popular with the launching of the **Remote Job Entry (RJE)**. This terminology is often used by major service providers such as IBM and DEC. Full-time sharing solutions were available on platforms such as Multics and Cambridge CTSS in the early 1970s. However, the *data center* model, which provides users with workstations on IBM mainframes and to send jobs to operators, was highly preferred.

In the 1990s, telecommunication companies, which previously provided data circuits from point to point, began offering high-quality VPN services at the same time as low-cost VPN services. VPN services can effectively use the overall network bandwidth while balancing server usage.

Cloud computing has contributed to the development of systems to cover all servers as well as network infrastructures. In the coming years, scientists and technology experts search for ways to provide more users with computers with large-scale computing power. CPUs have tried various algorithms and systems to prioritize the transaction sequence and to increase and optimize their efficiency. The use of the concept of the cloud for virtualized services may have been started by General Magic in 1994.

In this chapter, we will learn about the following topics:

- Cloud engine models
- Some of the cloud services
- Cronjob
- Storing data and creating schedule jobs for web scraping

Cloud engine models

The service-oriented architect evaluates **everything as a service (EaaS, XaaS or AAS)**. Cloud computing providers offer *services* in various formats: **Infrastructure as a Service (IaaS)**, **Platform as a Service (PaaS)** and **Software as a Service (SaaS)**. In the following part, we are going to talk about those formats.

Infrastructure as a service (IaaS)

IaaS includes online services designed to respond to various low-level details of network infrastructure, such as physical computing resources, location, data segmentation, scaling, security, backup, and top-level APIs.

Linux containers work in isolated sections of a single Linux kernel running directly on physical hardware. Linux groups and namespaces are used to isolate, secure, and manage containers.

In addition, container capacity is automatically scaled with the calculation load, which eliminates the overprovisioning problem and provides usage-based billing.

Platform as a service (PaaS)

PaaS is a cloud service where service providers offer users the hardware and software tools that are usually required for the application development over the internet.

Providers have hardware and software in their own infrastructure. PaaS thus saves users the trouble of installing hardware and software to develop or run a new application.

Software as a service (SaaS)

SaaS systems are providing an environment that is usually priced on a usage basis or on a subscription-fee basis. In addition, users have the ability to access cloud computing systems on their computers, using advanced computers, without having to install and maintain complex systems.

The SaaS applications model is typically priced as a monthly or a yearly fixed fee per user. Prices can be scaled and adjusted if a new user is added or removed. A disadvantage of SaaS is that users' data is stored in the cloud provider's server.

Mobile backend as a service (MBaaS)

Services include user management, push notifications, integration with social networking services, and more. This is a new pattern in cloud computing, and although most BaaS initiatives came after 2011, trends show that these services have gained a major traction power with corporate consumers.

Function as a service (FaaS)

FaaS takes advantage of serverless computing to enable the distribution of individual functions that are running in response to events. FaaS is not included in a broader range of server information, but terms can be used interchangeably.

Some of the cloud services

In this part, we are going to talk about two well-known and mostly preferred cloud services that are Google Cloud Compute Engine and Amazon Web Services.

Amazon Web Services (AWS)

The AWS platform emerged in July, 2002, initially consisting of only a few different vehicles and services. Later in late 2003, Chris Pinkham and Benjamin Black announced that the AWS concept would be reformatted when they offered an Amazon article explaining a vision for a fully standardized, fully automated retail storage infrastructure and applying it intensively to web services such as storage and retrieval.

By offering access to virtual servers as a service, they are encouraging the company to generate revenue from its new infrastructure investment. In November, 2004, the first AWS service for general use: **Simple Queue Service (SQS)** was released. After that, Pinkham and Christopher Brown developed an Amazon EC2 service in Cape Town, South Africa.

Amazon Web Services, Amazon S3 cloud storage, SQS, and combined version of EC2 were presented to the users on March 14, 2006.

Google Cloud

The Google Cloud Platform offered by Google is a cloud computing services package that operates on the same infrastructure that Google uses internally for end-user products such as Google Search and YouTube. In addition to a range of management tools, it also offers a range of modular cloud services, such as data processing, data storage, data analysis, and machine learning.

Google Cloud Platform offers users services infrastructure, PaaS, and computing environments without a server.

Cronjob

Cron is a work timer that is used in Unix-like computer operating systems. Developers can use cron for jobs that need to be run regularly at specific times, dates, or intervals. Briefly, the main idea behind using cronjob is automating system maintenance or management.

Cron is one of the most appropriate solutions for planning repetitive tasks. Cron is managed by a configuration file that specifies shell commands for a crontab (cron table) to run periodically in a particular program. Crontab files are stored where work lists and other instructions given to the cron daemon are stored. Users can have their own individual crontab files and are usually only found in the cron files or /etc subdirectory.

The syntax for each line is a cron expression consisting of five fields, followed by a shell command to execute.

For example, assuming the following cron default shell is compatible with the Bourne shell, Apache clears the error log every day after midnight (02:00):

```
0 2 * * * printf "" > /var/log/apache/error_log
```

This example runs the program that is called export_dump.sh at 21:30 (9:30 PM) every Saturday.

```
30 21 * * 6 /home/oracle/scripts/export_dump.sh
```

A user's configuration file can also be edited by calling crontab -e, regardless of where the actual application is stored. Some cron applications support non-standard macros specified in the following table:

Time	Definition	Cron
@yearly	Once, at midnight, on January 1 of each year	0 0 1 1 *
@monthly	Once, at midnight, on the first day of each month	0 0 1 * *
@weekly	Once, at midnight, on Sunday	0 0 * * 0
@daily	Once, every day, at midnight	0 0 * * *
@hourly	Once, at the beginning of every hour	0 * * * *

Storing data and creating schedule jobs for web scraping

In this part, we are going to create a free-tier AWS RDS instance and write a script to connect this database by using the RPostgreSQL library. After writing this script, we will create a cronjob that automatizes web scraping and sending data to the database based on the scheduled time.

Creating an AWS RDS Instance

Let's take a look at how to create the PostgreSQL database on AWS. In this section, we will talk about how to create an AWS account and how to create an RDS instance step by step:

1. First, visit the AWS page by using the following URL: https://aws.amazon.com/

2. Then click **My Account** to go to the login screen, as shown in the following screenshot:

AWS main page

3. Click the **AWS Management Console**, and then you will see the following page about logging in or signing up
4. Put in your email address, which you would like to create an AWS account with and click **Create a new AWS account**:

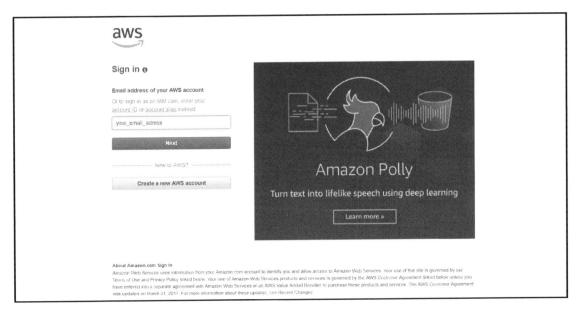

AWS Management Console

5. After creating your account, you will be able to use the AWS services by logging into your AWS account.

6. Click the **Services** tab, find the RDS under the database section, and click it to create an RDS instance:

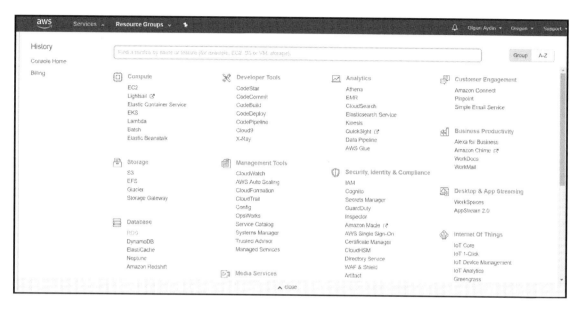

List of AWS services

7. Click the **Instances** tab on the left menu. As shown in following screenshot, we can see the RDS Instances, which I already have.

8. After creating instances, it's time to create a database. To do this, you can use the **Create Database** button:

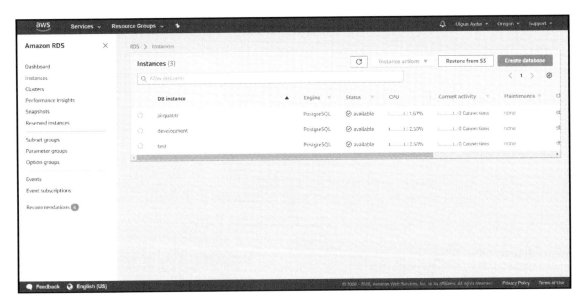

AWS console

9. This section is for selecting a type of database. Because we would like to create a PostgreSQL database, we are going to select **PostgreSQL**:

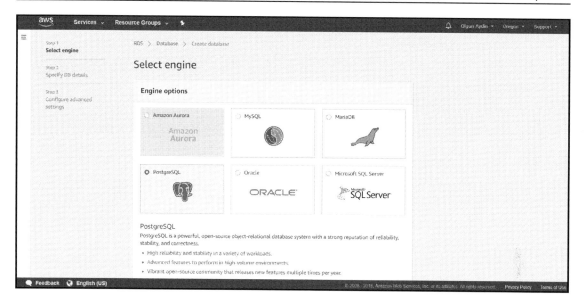

Creating an RDS Instance Step 1

10. Now it's time to specify the database details. You can decide the licence model and the database engine version from the following screen:

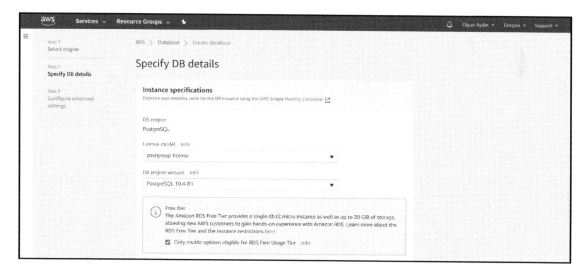

Creating an RDS Instance Step 2

11. From the following section, you can specify the database instance class, storage type, and allocated storage:

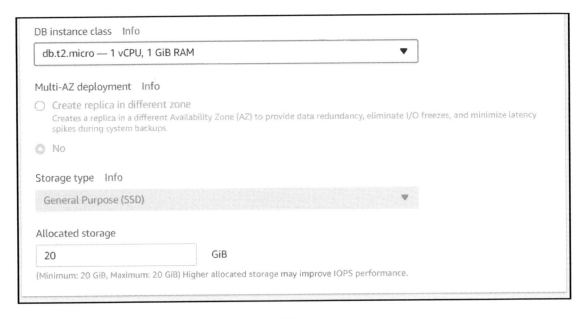

Creating an RDS Instance Step 3

12. From the last section, you can define identifier for your database, username, and password.

13. To complete creating an AWS RDS Instance Process, we can go to the next page by clicking the **Next** button:

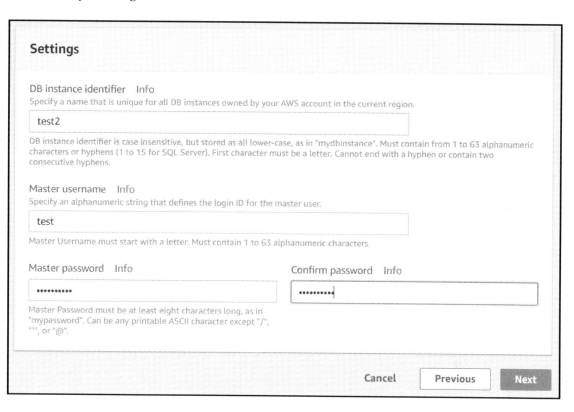

Creating an RDS Instance Step 4

14. The last step is adding a name to your database. You can assign a name to your database as shown here:

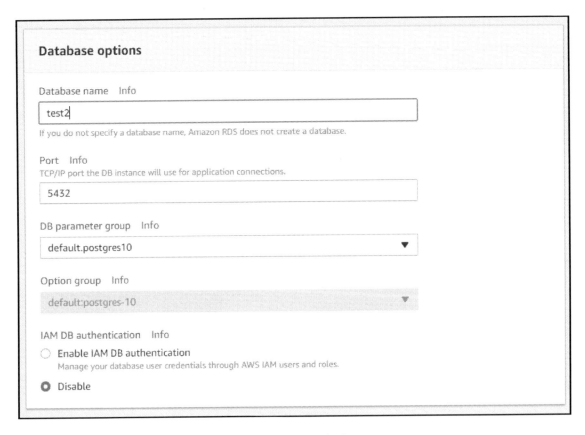

Creating an RDS Instance Step 5

Connecting to the PostgreSQL database on AWS

In this section, we are going to talk about how to connect a PostgreSQL database on AWS by using the RPostgreSQL library. If you don't have this library on your R environment, you can install it by using the following command:

```
install.packages("RPostgreSQL")
```

- Sign into your AWS account, and click **Instances** from the left menu, as shown in the following screenshot:

Dashboard for an RDS Instance, which is called development

- Scroll down to the **Details** section and then find the endpoint:

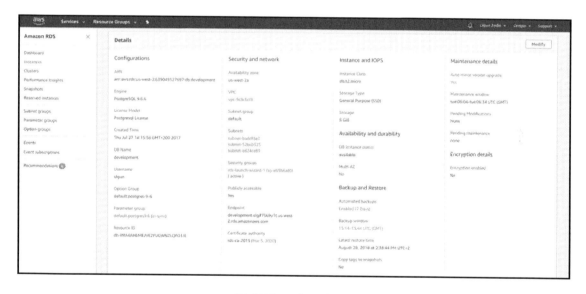

List of details regarding your instance

- Now we can connect to the PostgreSQL database using the endpoint mentioned here: `development.clgjf7569y1t.us-west-2.rds.amazonaws.com`

When you are connecting your own database, please be sure that you are using correct endpoint.

- Let's use R to connect to the database.
- Most important, we need to install the RPostgreSQL package. We will use the install.packages() command, and we will then be able to install the package directly:

```
> install.packages("RPostgreSQL")
```

- Then, the next step will be calling the package by using a library() command:

```
> library("RPostgreSQL")
```

- We will then do a setup to connect to the PostgreSQL DB using R. We are loading RPostgreSQL driver and using it in the following step to connect to the DB:

```
drv <- dbDriver("PostgreSQL")
```

- When we use the DB driver, earlier stored in a drv variable, we can then connect to the PostgreSQL DB by using the following R commands.
- We are going to connect test2 database which we have created
- Make sure that you are using the variable to store the connection for querying

```
con <- dbConnect(drv, dbname = "test2",

host = "endpointofyourinstance",port=5432,user= "username",
password = "pass"
```

We have learned how to connect to a PostgreSQL database using R.

- Let's create an R script that scraps the web page and stores this data to the database on AWS.

As you remember, we have already written the following script to scrap devveri (http://devveri.com/). We are going to use the same script to collect data, but we will be just adding a block of scripts to connect db and store data on db:

```
#loading library
library(rvest)

#creating NULL variables
name <- NULL
date <- NULL
comment_count <- NULL

#links for page
urls <- "http://devveri.com/"

#reading main url
h <- read_html(urls)

#getting names
n<- html_nodes(h, xpath =
'/html/body/div[3]/div/div[1]/div/h2/a/text()')

#getting dates
d<- html_nodes(h, xpath =
'/html/body/div[3]/div/div[1]/div/p[1]/span[1]/text()')

#getting comment counts
comc<- html_nodes(h, xpath =
'/html/body/div[3]/div/div[1]/div/p[1]/span[4]/a/text()')

#saving results
name<- as.matrix(as.character(n))
date<- as.matrix(as.character(d))
comment_count <- as.matrix(as.character(comc))

#creating final data frame
final_data <- data.frame(name, comment_count, date)
```

- We will need to load the library.

```
library("RPostgreSQL")
```

- To connect a database via R, we are going to load the PostgreSQL driver to the R environment, because we have the PostgreSQL database.

```
#load db driver
drv <- dbDriver("PostgreSQL")
```

- We can connect to the database by using the following command. To do it, we have to use the dbConnect function. In this function, we are defining the database name, host(endpoint on AWS), username, and password:

```
#connecting to db
con <-dbConnect(drv,dbname = "test2",host = "endpointofyourinstance",
port = 5432,user = "user",password = "pass")
```

- Then, let's store our final data frame to the database. To do this, we are using dbWriteTable function. First, we are defining the connection that we stored to the con variable.
- Then, we are defining our database table name, which is going to be devveri:

```
#writing final dataframes to the table
dbWriteTable(con, "devveri", final_data, row.names = FALSE,
append = TRUE)
```

We have created an R script to collect data from the devveri.com and store the data to the PostgreSQL database, which is hosted on AWS.

Creating cronjob

As we discussed, cronjobs are for scheduling a task and automatizing scripts. They are triggering scripts based on your preferences. For example, if you have a daily cronjob, this job will trigger the script/scripts on a daily basis.

Creating cronjobs on Linux-based operation systems is quite easy and straightforward. But on windows, this would be a bit hard and more complicated. Don't worry; R Studio already thought about this, and it has released scheduler add-in for this purpose.

- To activate and use scheduler add-in, please click **Tools** on RStudio and mouse over **Addins** and then click **Browse Addins**:

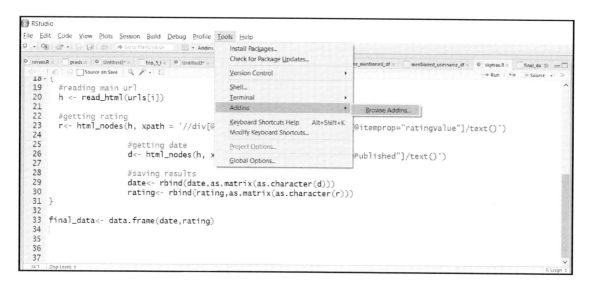

R Studio Tools Menu

- After clicking **Browse Addins**, you will see the screen that is shown on the following screenshot.

- Click **taskscheduleR** and click **Execute** to schedule tasks on R:

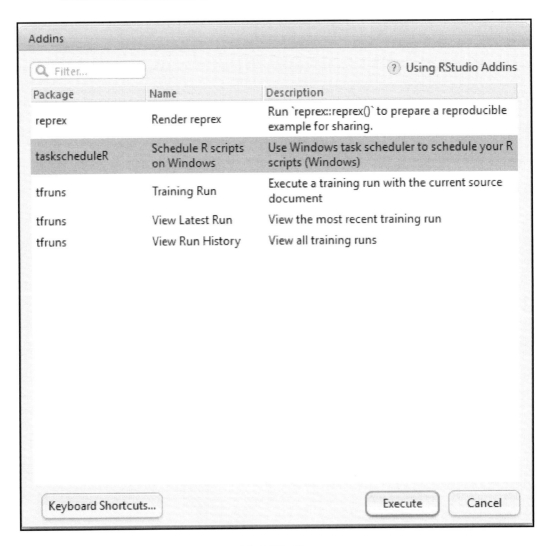

R Studio Addins Menu

- Afterward, you are able to see **Taskscheduler** under the **Addins** section:

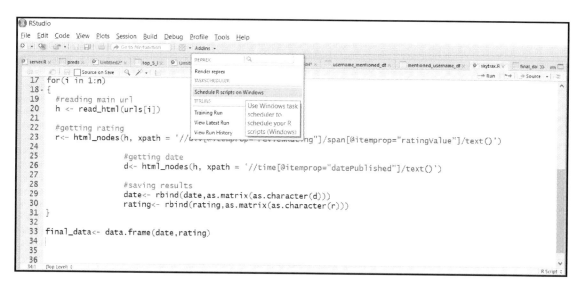

Reaching installed add-ins on RStudio

- When you click **taskscheduler**, you will see this screen
- To schedule a script, you should upload this script file using **Browse**
- You can select frequency from **Schedule** part

- You can also define start date and time.

Interface of Task Scheduler Add-in

Summary

In this chapter, we focused on the fundamentals of cloud computing. We have learned how to create AWS Instances and how to connect PostgreSQL database, which is hosted on AWS, by using R. Finally, we focused on creating cronjobs on R. Now you are able to create end-to-end web scraping system by using R.

In this book, we covered main topics regarding web scraping with R. We talked about the main idea behind web scraping, learned how Regex rules work, and learned how to use XPath rules and how to write them. We have created our first web-scraping script using the rvest library and even created a graph, using collected data.

Finally, we discussed about Selenium. Using the RSelenium library, we created a web scrapper on top of R. Then, we took a look at how to store the data we collected and how to schedule our web-scraping tools on R.

So, now you are ready to build your own web scrapers using R! Don't forget to store the data and schedule your tasks!

Other Books You May Enjoy

If you enjoyed this book, you may be interested in these other books by Packt:

Machine Learning with R - Second Edition
Brett Lantz

ISBN: 978-1-78439-390-8

- Harness the power of R to build common machine learning algorithms with real-world data science applications
- Get to grips with R techniques to clean and prepare your data for analysis, and visualize your results
- Discover the different types of machine learning models and learn which is best to meet your data needs and solve your analysis problems
- Classify your data with Bayesian and nearest neighbor methods
- Predict values by using R to build decision trees, rules, and support vector machines
- Forecast numeric values with linear regression, and model your data with neural networks
- Evaluate and improve the performance of machine learning models
- Learn specialized machine learning techniques for text mining, social network data, big data, and more

Machine Learning with R Cookbook
Yu-Wei, Chiu (David Chiu)

ISBN: 978-1-78398-204-2

- Create and inspect the transaction dataset, performing association analysis with the Apriori algorithm
- Visualize patterns and associations using a range of graphs and find frequent itemsets using the Eclat algorithm
- Compare differences between each regression method to discover how they solve problems
- Predict possible churn users with the classification approach
- Implement the clustering method to segment customer data
- Compress images with the dimension reduction method
- Incorporate R and Hadoop to solve machine learning problems on big data

Leave a review - let other readers know what you think

Please share your thoughts on this book with others by leaving a review on the site that you bought it from. If you purchased the book from Amazon, please leave us an honest review on this book's Amazon page. This is vital so that other potential readers can see and use your unbiased opinion to make purchasing decisions, we can understand what our customers think about our products, and our authors can see your feedback on the title that they have worked with Packt to create. It will only take a few minutes of your time, but is valuable to other potential customers, our authors, and Packt. Thank you!

Index

Printed in Great Britain
by Amazon